WIRED FOR LIFE

Dedicated to the present,
this moment in which anything is possible.

WIRED FOR LIFE

>RETRAIN YOUR BRAIN AND THRIVE

MARTINA SHEEHAN AND SUSAN PEARSE

Published and distributed in Australia by: Hay House Australia Pty. Ltd.: www.hayhouse.com.au
Published and distributed in the United States by: Hay House, Inc.: www.hayhouse.com
Published and distributed in the United Kingdom by: Hay House UK, Ltd.: www.hayhouse.co.uk
Published and distributed in South Africa by: Hay House SA (Pty), Ltd.: www.hayhouse.co.za
Distributed in Canada by: Raincoast: www.raincoast.com
Published in India by: Hay House Publishers India: www.hayhouse.co.in

Design by Rhett Nacson
Typeset by Simon Paterson
Edited by Margie Tubbs

ISBN: 978-1-4019-3850-5
Digital ISBN: 978-1-4019-3376-0

15 14 13 12   5 4 3 2
1st edition, October 2012
2nd edition, December 2012

Printed in Australia by McPherson's Printing Group

> Contents

introduction   vii

chapter one   do you thrive or just survive?   1

chapter two   your mind is a garden   11

chapter three   the fear of failure: it's time to take a chance   33

chapter four   the fear of losing control: it's time to let it go   49

chapter five   the fear of standing out: it's time to find your voice   69

chapter six   the fear of missing out: it's time to think abundantly   89

chapter seven   the fear of facing the truth: it's time to take responsibility   107

chapter eight   how to get wired for life   123

chapter nine   wake up   147

chapter ten   think differently   167

chapter eleven   grow   189

chapter twelve   thriving not just surviving   207

appendix 1   seven-day mind work-out   215

appendix 2   traps that lie in wait   221

references   227
resources   231
testimonials   235
acknowledgements   237

> introduction

> Are you ready to get 'Wired for Life'? Many years ago we certainly were. We both remember 'waking up' and realising that we had success without fulfilment, freedom without happiness, activity without authenticity. In that moment of realisation, we both knew that it was time to think differently and find a way to live differently. We took the usual path through new hobbies and interests, classes on this and that, new places to live, new jobs to try, new people to see. And we still had a yearning gap.

Then luck threw us a curve ball and we caught it. We sat facing the truth, not for the first time in our lives, but this time we saw it, heard it, and finally acknowledged it. We were holding ourselves back and it didn't matter where we lived, who we lived with, what we did or what we had accumulated. As always, our mind took the lead but it was full of fears, half-truths, bad habits and tricks. Once we looked inside we saw the trap, but also the way out.

We are two people with different personalities but, like everybody else, we ultimately seek the same things: to appreciate our lives, to be happy with our choices, and to feel like we are making some sort of difference. We want to experience a life well lived. At that time, we faced different obstacles and had different ways of reacting to what life put in our path, yet we both emerged with the same answer. We'd like to share with you our personal stories and show you how our journey led to the lives we are living now.

› introducing susan pearse

I feel lucky to have had a very normal upbringing, raised by loving parents who to this day are still together and happy. I grew up in a small town that fostered a real sense of community. I was ticking off the checklist that should lead to happiness and success. Many amazing friends. Tick. Great school. Tick. Great grades. Tick. The right type of attention from the right boys. Tick. I seemed to be on the right track.

After leaving school I entered the university program that was my first preference, got an amazing job straight out of uni, worked hard, got promoted, and in no time was managing people two and three times my age.

I had the dream wedding to a perfect guy, we were on track to pay off our mortgage in under five years, and had planned when our first baby would be due. I always knew where and when my next vacation would be and when my next promotion was due. My days were scheduled, my weekends were organised, in fact my whole life was planned. And I achieved everything I set out to do. From the outside, people would have said I was a high achiever who had it all together. But if I didn't have a picture in my head of what something was 'supposed' to be like and a plan to get there, I felt lost, uneasy, fearful.

Then one day as I was following my plans to live happily ever after, I woke up. Not just literally but metaphorically. I felt a deep sense of emptiness. I felt trapped, unhappy and unfulfilled. On the surface I had ticked all the boxes and had everything I needed, but life had no meaning and I was miserable. I had been following life's path, or at least the path that everyone told me I needed to follow, but I awoke to find this path was not for me. I felt there was a bigger purpose that I was missing. But how would I find it? I had no idea what I liked, wanted or believed in. I realised that for 28 years I had lived like a robot, giving little thought to anything except the next step in the plan.

I had no idea who I was but I knew one thing: waking up was frightening, because losing the plan meant stepping into the unknown. For someone so attached to being in control, this looming void left me paralysed. I didn't act, I just kept going through the motions and fighting the feeling. But sooner or later something had to give. Unfortunately everything that was familiar and comfortable to me gave way at the same time. My marriage, my house, my job and my life as I knew it were all gone within months. At the time it scared the life out of me, but I now look back on it as the most precious moment, my turning point. I was finally in a position to really learn what my life was all about. And this was when I reconnected with someone from my past who was on the same search as me: someone who was to become a significant part of my future life's purpose.

› introducing martina sheehan

I also had a very normal upbringing in a happy family. Eight years younger than my closest sibling, I almost had the life of an only child, and it made me fairly independent. I found my life unremarkable, but I suppose on reflection it was not a particularly normal path for a young girl. When people asked me what I wanted to be when I grew up, I always answered 'An astronaut!' I had my pilot's licence before my driver's licence and studied mechanical engineering at university. I was the only girl in a class of guys for four years. It was great fun and I ambled along through life without much thought. Yes there were some stumbling blocks, like failing a subject and repeating, but none of this really concerned me. I was supported by a wonderful family who provided me with the tools to take responsibility for my life without feeling pressured or judged. But I never had a plan.

Going with the flow became my strength but also my trap. Without a sense of purpose or direction, I too easily slipped into the traditional roles in life: job with a big company, engaged at 24, buying our first house at 25. But I should have known that the picture of career, marriage and kids was never for me. The signs had been there all along. I was a non-conformist, but I was the only one who didn't see it. I was never rebellious; but I now know that my gut, my instinct or whatever you might want to call it, had been trying to wake me up for a long time and I wasn't listening. Just a few years out of university while plodding along as an engineer, I was asked to take on the challenge of establishing a new unit in the human resources group of an organisation with 20,000 people. Strange I thought, but why not? And somehow I knew I was on the right track. Engineering was never my thing, but people were fascinating!

My life then became a series of steps moving away from dissatisfaction, but I was not clear what I was moving towards. I broke off the engagement and started my own consulting business. But I still hadn't found my purpose or my voice. My real moment of waking up and taking a long hard look at myself was really just an accumulation of moments. Yes, it happened suddenly one day in a crumpled ball of tears over some useless guy, but that was just the final grain of sand landing on a precarious pile that had been ready to fall for a while. I had not been listening closely enough to the increasingly strident calls from inside and now it gave one final 'Hey!' and I remember saying 'Okay, I know nothing. What now?' I was finally ready to start designing my own path through life.

> following the path

We didn't find our answers immediately. We both wanted to make a difference in a way we felt we weren't currently doing, so we started a business together. We tried meditation. We stretched our bodies with yoga and our brains with science, anthropology, and philosophy. We read and read and read. But something was still missing inside. We needed to do something uplifting, something that would truly provide us with much needed inspiration. It was clear; we needed to go shopping in New York City!

For Susan, having followed the path of the disciplined planner, overseas travel came second to paying off bills. She had only been overseas once for her Fijian honeymoon. Fifth Avenue was definitely calling. And like most business owners who needed to travel over to the other side of the world, we wanted to make it cost-effective. So we decided to look for a work conference we could attend. We scrolled the register. Biotech in NYC? No, that wouldn't work. Then there it was, *Investigating the Mind* in Boston. The same dates we wanted to travel and Boston wasn't far from New York City. If it wasn't interesting, we could always just grab the conference papers and continue our journey toward bright shiny objects. Done! Unfortunately general admissions were sold out, but we calculated it would be worth our while to attend as gold sponsors. It wasn't long before we were on our way.

We arrived at the conference and shopping was soon off the agenda when we realised who was lined up before us in the gold sponsor admission area. Richard Gere! That's right. The one and only, and he looks better in real life than he does on the big screen. We followed him in a trance-like state and strategically positioned ourselves so we could maintain full view of his glorious visage. But very soon something much more important stole our attention away. The conference was a dialogue between the world's leading neuroscientists and Buddhist monks, including the Dalai Lama. They were exploring the emerging research on the brain and how this information could shine a light on practical ways for people to cultivate positive emotions.

It was mesmerising information and it shifted our way of thinking overnight. What we take for granted in our lives is not set, predetermined or 'just the way I am'. Every thought, emotion and action is a choice; you just might not be making that choice consciously. And when you are not choosing consciously, your brain can only follow its well-worn patterns, habits and default pathways. Being on autopilot was our problem and now we saw that, unless we switched autopilot off and ourselves back on, we could never expect permanent change in our lives. It was not enough to wake up once, we needed to make waking up our new habit. Otherwise life would keep giving us a gentle push or a hard slap until we started paying attention.

Since that day in 2003 we have followed the emerging research on the human mind, translating it into simple principles that explain why we think, feel and act as we do. And more importantly, we've identified the essential steps and practical ways to create the only habits you need in your life: to wake up, to think differently and to grow.

We started with our own minds and we refined our approach through our own experiences. Susan let go of her plans, over-preparation and need to control and emerged as a person who values people over getting things done. Martina found her voice and emerged as a person always ready to offer a fresh perspective and a calm guiding hand.

We immediately knew this was our life's work and that we had finally uncovered our purpose—not just for our business but also in our lives. We exist to cultivate consciousness. This simple statement guides everything we do and has provided us with the sense of meaning that had been missing up to that point.

We had hundreds of ideas on how the research could be translated to help the everyday person. We developed products, programs and strategies to help businesses achieve success by thinking differently. We were already working in organisational consulting, so it made sense to start where we were. We transformed leaders, teams, cultures, relationships and businesses themselves with this unique approach. Our business, reinvention® (www.reinvention.com.au) is still going strong in its second decade.

Many of our clients asked us to create something that would help them stay on track and share what they had learnt with their families, so our next venture was to make our programs accessible to individuals. We created Mind Gardener® in 2009 (www.mindgardener.com). Offering programs and tools to help people stick with their daily commitment to cultivate their mind has been just one more way that we hope to contribute to a world that is starting to wake up to the full potential of the human mind.

In our own lives in recent years there have been new and happy relationships formed, children born, and world travel experiences pursued. This decade was not necessarily any different in terms of the twists and turns that life throws us all, but it was certainly approached and lived with greater clarity, authenticity, freedom and happiness.

Our first book, *Wired for Life*, is a culmination of our work over the last decade. In it we share the secrets for thriving in your life. You will find many people's stories (in which the names have been changed) and maybe you will recognise yourself in their experiences. It's the book we needed many years ago. We hope it inspires you to take the leap and get wired for life too.

› susan and martina: a quick (but important) aside.

The conference that started as a shopping trip had changed our lives and the path that we would take. But the life-changing moments didn't end there. On the last day we were advised that His Holiness the Dalai Lama would like to have a private audience with the handful of gold sponsors. With Richard Gere just an arm's length away, we bowed our heads and had a special few moments with His Holiness.

› do you thrive or just survive?

› And there it was. My friend's first Facebook status update for the week: 'Is it wrong to be wishing it's the weekend on a Monday morning?' But it wasn't so much the status update that was the big surprise. It was the 32 comments that said 'No, that is totally normal. That's what we are all doing.'

It is astounding what is considered normal. Being stressed out, hating your job, struggling through life and wishing you were somewhere else. We see too many people fall into this trap, and it *is* a trap. Life does not have to be difficult. Life's circumstances may be hard, but how you choose to respond to them is completely in your hands. Life is what you make it, and we all fall into the trap at some time in our life of making it difficult.

Do you thrive or do you just survive? Every day we see people move mechanically through their lives. At first glance they appear successful, but there's clearly something missing. They may seem distracted or lost, tense or deflated, distant or purposeless. You can't always put your finger on it, but you can sense their dissatisfaction with life.

We met Eddie at a seminar about five years ago, when he was the Chief Executive Officer of a medium-sized automotive company.

He was young, enthusiastic and forward thinking. His team found him to be an inspirational leader. Shortly after we met him, he was headhunted for the most prized role in his industry. It put him in charge of a very large international company and brought him wealth, position and the lifestyle to match. He moved his family to a new house in a prestigious inner city suburb, mixed in all the right circles, and earned lots of frequent flyer points. Still in his 30s, it would be difficult for anyone to label him anything other than successful. But Eddie didn't feel that way. It's not that he wanted more, he just realised that he wanted, well, *something* and he wasn't sure what. He persevered for three years and over that time we saw him become unhappier, unhealthier and less enthusiastic about his role. Then one day it all unravelled. The job was gone and Eddie moved out of the family home. Today Eddie is in a deep personal search to find that missing something.

We had been there ourselves and we wanted some answers. Why do we accept mere survival for so long without question? What is this trap that tightens its grip and holds us back? Why, when we've tried so hard to loosen its hold, do we still feel like we're not quite there? What's the secret for living a good life?

› a life well lived

The ultimate success is surely a well-lived life in all its forms. For each of us this means something different. But the satisfaction that you have been your very best as a friend, as a parent, a partner and a worker might just be the greatest reward. In fact your brain's reward centres light up when you are able to fully realise your potential and be the person you wish to be without something holding you back.

The concept of a life well lived is universally appealing, but it's a concept that conjures up different things for us all. Just like beauty, it's in the eye of the beholder. You may look at another person and say 'Ah, that's the life' and your friend counters with 'I wouldn't want to be them.'

We all tend to see pictures in our head of the way we'd like our lives to unfold. A parent may see happy children gathered around the dinner table, laughing and sharing stories. In business you may see recognition by peers, bosses and clients. A sportsperson sees a win, an artist sees acclaim. You may see a lifestyle, a place where you aspire to live or the perfect partner to spend your life with. Our descriptions are likely to be as varied and unique as our appearances. I may wish for the same pace of life as you but I may wish to live it in France, while your picture has you in your original family home. We may all wish for our children to be happy, but one person sees this in terms of career success while another sees them enjoying the freedom of travel. But the feeling we seek is universal. We all ultimately want to feel fulfilled, happy and complete.

Why then do we make decisions that steer us away from our picture? Why do we make choices that limit us? Why do we look life in the face and falter when it places an opportunity at our feet?

We were particularly interested in the people who seemed to have it all together. We thought *we* did, then suddenly it unravelled. The fact that people can seem to have it all but still feel empty, frustrated, disappointed and alone is a mystery, and it was one we wanted to solve. We can all point to people who are rich but unhappy. People who have travelled the world, but still feel lost; people who are famous, yet end up in rehab; people who have status, but are chronically lonely. And people who have all of the resources at their fingertips, but still fail to create a life where success also means fulfilment and happiness.

If you believe that there is something you need to get, something more to have, something in your life to change, or someone who can fix it for you, you will continue to come up short. Research on how the brain processes happiness shows that only 10 per cent of your happiness can be attributed to material factors or life circumstances. So you're looking in the wrong direction if you are searching for some return from external factors.

Fifty per cent of your happiness can be attributed to something called the 'happiness set point'. Studies show that, even after winning the lottery, an initial period of elation is followed by a return to the happiness set point a short time later. This 50 per cent is believed to be genetic. The only studies that show permanent changes to this portion are those conducted with Buddhist monks who have made meditation their life's work.

The remaining 40 per cent of your happiness can be attributed to your choices and intentional activities. Sonja Lyubomirsky, a well-regarded happiness researcher, says the 40 per cent can be changed by '... what we do and how we think'.[1]

So there it is. The trap has been sitting inside you all along. And so has the answer. You can spend years searching, only to find the journey will bring you back to yourself. Until you realise that achieving your version of the life well lived requires you to pay attention to your own mind, you will be lost in a continuous spin, looking for the answers everywhere else and finding that your solutions are short-lived. We see people trying a new hobby, a new job, a new country, a new partner, then finding themselves in the same boat all over again.

The way you think wires your brain and determines everything you feel, say and do. In particular, your brain has natural default patterns and biases that were designed to serve your survival. And they do this so well that they promote surviving at the expense of thriving. Patterns like avoiding risk, holding on too tight, pushing people away, and failing to take responsibility trip people up over and over again. We thought it was time people knew the truth. Because understanding why, how and when these patterns will rise up and swallow your dreams is the first step in getting wired for life.

› looks can be deceiving

I have three words that will send shivers down your spine: High School Reunion! It's one of those events in life designed to trigger a dose of self-doubt. The burning question is 'What will they think of me now?' Everyone is checking each other out and forming a view.

Brett, Jodie, Sarah, Bill and Amanda all went to my high school. Twenty years later we were gathered in the school hall taking a good hard look at each other. As I looked around, I felt happy for them all. They appeared to have great lives. But I also knew that looks can be deceiving. Were these the very people who carried around the lurking traps that play in the mind of seemingly successful people?

As our discussions deepened over the next few hours, it became clear that this was definitely the case. Life was not a bed of roses and it was not unfolding as any of them had expected. They pointed to many different reasons for their disappointments, but none of them could see the real trap.

› the search for success

v   v   v   v   v

› Brett was still a good-looking guy. At school he was captain of the footy team and this made him one of the popular kids. Years later, he'd traded his footy uniform for a suit and held a senior role in a prestigious advertising company. He had a very impressive client list and seemed to take pride in dropping the names of some well-known figures around town. He was proud of the life he had built for his family: best suburb, best schools, great holidays. And he was still popular. Old mates flocked to shake his hand and the girls waved and flirted. As the night wore on, Brett revealed a secret. He was not doing what he loved and he felt trapped. He had many excuses for why he could not change direction now and he ended our conversation that night saying 'It's just a pipe dream. We've got a good life and I wouldn't want to lose that.' Brett had succumbed to the fear of failure and it was holding him back from taking a chance to do something he really loved.

^ ^ ^ ^ ^

› the search for freedom

∨ ∨ ∨ ∨ ∨

› Jodie had always known where she was heading in life and her life had followed that plan nicely. We'd always joked that she was a control freak but it seemed to have worked for her so far. She was a successful accountant in a big firm and had quickly made Partner. She had travelled widely during her early 20s and met the perfect guy at 27, right on target. They were married three years later and had worked hard to get themselves comfortably established before considering kids. And her first had arrived just eight months before this reunion. I was impressed that she could get out of the house in such lovely designer clothes without a mark on them! Jodie happily showed all her friends some lovely photos of her daughter but as we talked, she let her guard down saying 'It's just so hard. I never thought it would be like this. Nothing seemed to work for ages but I've finally got her doing everything to a perfect schedule. It takes a lot to keep that working but I couldn't handle it any other way. I can't remember the last time I felt relaxed.' And as she told me this I could see the frustration, exhaustion, stress and determination play across her face. Jodie had developed a fear of losing control and she had no idea how to let go and enjoy life.

^ ^ ^ ^ ^

› the search for authenticity

v v v v v

› Sarah had always been a bit different. She had been hard to get to know at school and not much seemed to have changed. Always the hippie, she had realised her dream of becoming an artist, but it was others who told me how good she really was. When I chatted with her later in the evening, she was very humble about her achievements and kept trying to change the topic and talk about me. When I asked her how she promoted her work she said it was all word of mouth 'But the problem with that is then people approach me and they want more than just a painting. They want me to talk at their gallery or to a group and I can't do that. I just want to stay in my workshop, but these days people want to know who you are and what you think. That's not my thing so it will always hold me back. I'll probably never make a real living out of it.' Sarah had a fear of standing out and, unless she found her voice, she would continue to undermine her own success.

^ ^ ^ ^ ^

› the search for fulfilment

v v v v v

› Bill had been very idealistic at school. He always took the high moral ground and was a keen debater. None of us were surprised when he went into political life and he had been a politician until very recently. He had retired from politics a few months ago and made a complete sea change. He'd moved his family to a quiet little beach town and bought the corner store. He looked more relaxed and healthy than I'd last seen him, which was on TV during the last election campaign. When I asked Bill if it was everything he'd hoped for he first gave me the politician's response 'Yes, it's fantastic. Best decision I ever made.' But then he alluded to some situations that were causing him some concern. 'Actually, it doesn't matter where you go or what you do, there's always someone out to get you. I thought I would be able to relax and just run the business, but even there it's dog eat dog. I've had a few battles and I've got a big one on my hands at the moment. But I'll win. I've got heaps of experience beating the competition!' Bill found it hard not to see every situation as a battle because that had been the norm in his political life. His search for fulfilment was being thwarted by his win/lose mentality and a fear of missing out.

^ ^ ^ ^ ^

› the search for happiness

ˇ ˇ ˇ ˇ ˇ

› Then there was Amanda. You couldn't help but notice her. Always impeccably dressed and made up, she was still vivacious and attractive. Amanda had always wanted the high life and had found the perfect guy to give it to her. As the night wore on, you could see people have a quick chat with her then move on, but Amanda looked confident and stood her ground expecting people to come to her. Eventually I went over to find out more about her life. 'I'm great,' she said. 'Divorced that bastard and I'm glad. Do you ever hear about him? He'll come to no good, I'll make sure of that. I'm not very impressed by this venue. Why didn't they have it somewhere nice? This wine is very average. And I can't see that anyone has really made it, know what I mean?' I could see why people had moved on quickly from Amanda. She had been divorced for five years and she was clearly still bitter and resentful. She hadn't moved on and seemed to be stuck with a victim mentality, not just about her failed marriage, but about everything. She needed to take responsibility for her life and face reality, if she was to ever find happiness again.

∧　∧　∧　∧　∧

› what can you do about it?

None of my old school friends realised that their own brains were tripping them up. They pointed to life circumstances as their excuse, but I could also see that each of them were starting to realise a change was needed. In the coming days they all separately made contact with me and suggested we get together. Although most of them disguised it as an invitation to simply reconnect and socialise, I could hear their desire to talk more about their lives. Something in our conversations at the reunion had made them reflect and wonder if there was more they could do to find that missing element in their lives. And I was happy to oblige. I'd been where they were and I knew that the door only has to crack slightly to let in a stream of light. I had already learnt that nothing but changing my own mindset had ever made a lasting difference in my life. Every time I forgot that I got lost again. This simple truth had changed my world and I could see each of them were just about ready to hear it.

So throughout this book we'll check in with these five friends. Each of them reveals a particular habit of mind that drove them away from their vision of a well-lived life. Understanding why they made decisions they regretted, made choices that limited them, and did things that were clearly not in their best interests may help you to better understand yourself and find a new way to achieve a life well lived.

So now, if you're ready to get wired for life and overcome the traps that might be holding you back, we need to introduce you to someone who is going to be critical to this journey: please meet your brain.

› your mind is a garden

› Do you think your life is a result of your circumstances or is it actually of your own making? Could it be that your own thoughts, beliefs, ideas, doubts, fears, preferences and decisions are tripping you up? It is becoming increasingly clear that what happens in our minds is directly translated into outcomes in our lives.

Nothing brought this home to us more than a story from a friend, after floods devastated parts of our home town, Brisbane. Many of the affected areas along the river are home to more affluent people, but of course, the river recognises no such distinctions and affects rich and poor the same. I was at a meeting a number of weeks after the floods and one of the participants told how her home went under, her possessions were ruined, and she was not covered by insurance. She ended her story saying 'But we are safe, I still have my job, and we can rebuild.' Another meeting participant told of a colleague in almost identical circumstances and of similar socio-economic standing. But the punch line in this story was different. That father had taken his own life, unable to cope with the loss of so much that had defined his existence.

It is not our circumstances that determine our path through life, it is how we respond to them. But all action starts first with a thought. When you start with the thought *it will be okay*, you act very differently than if you start with the thought *there is no hope*. Each thought is the first step on a different path. We spend so much time considering how we should act, but we would be better off spending this time considering how we should think.

› the source of all thinking

Many of us would have learnt the basics about our body, but who ever learnt about their brain? We often ask this question in workshops and occasionally a hand or two will go up. Inevitably they have studied psychology or done a personal exploration of the increasingly accessible neuroscience research. But it tends to end there. Isn't it amazing that the one part of your anatomy that directs and controls every other part, and interprets your every life experience, should continue to be such a mystery? And it is even more amazing that we don't even stop to wonder about it.

Just as a growing understanding about the human body and its need for nutrition, exercise and rest has empowered you to make better choices about your health, an understanding of the workings of your brain will transform the way in which you approach your relationships, your work, and every experience in your life. The last frontier of human exploration sits inside you.

› an exciting discovery in science

We are entering the age of the brain. Until the last 20 years, the popular view was that the adult brain, once formed, did not fundamentally change (except to decline in old age!). Since the advent of technology that has enabled scientists to see the brain in action in real time, it has become overwhelmingly clear that your brain has the potential to continue changing and adapting throughout life. And notice we use the word 'potential'. It also has the potential to become rigid and constrained. It is completely up to you whether the potential of your brain is optimised.

The science of neuroplasticity (the ability of the brain to change structurally and functionally in response to its environment) explains that everything you think, learn, see and do shapes your brain and changes your life. You will literally finish each day with a brain that is different than it was in the morning. In fact, when you finish reading this page your brain will be different. Literally.

We get excited by the idea that, one day, you might be able to walk through a contraption a bit like an airport security scanner and see an image of your brain as it is at that moment. Then later, after you've attended a lecture, met a friend for lunch, played with the kids after school, or done a day's work, you wander back through the scanner and get a second image. In what way did your experiences change your brain during that hour or that day? And in what way do these changes influence your thoughts, feelings and behaviours?

Discussing science, when what you really want to think about is how to change your life, might sound pretty dry. But it is actually the most empowering discovery of our times! To realise that this mysterious and complex organ, that could fit in your hands and weighs only 1.5 kg, holds the secret to understanding yourself and others in ways you never thought could be so simple and obvious, is truly a doorway to a new life, and a whole new world.

And this is not an idle promise. We've lived it and we've seen it over and over again in ourselves and others: how a simple fact about the brain can make sense of the way you react to a situation and, in recognising this, can reveal an alternative that transforms your life.

v v v v v

› Brett had been a carefree guy at school. About one year ago, his wife had a health scare and he found himself becoming a compulsive worrier. On a daily basis, he worried that her condition might return and that she might not be able to get medical help in time. But beyond that, he felt like he had started to worry more about everything in his life: losing his family, losing his job, losing his lifestyle.

Everything you think shapes your brain. Brett had literally been training himself to worry for the last 12 months. Just like training a muscle in your body, if you practise a thought repetitively over a period of time, it will get stronger and stronger. This is neuroplasticity in practice. Brett had created a well-worn neural pathway of worry, and it was very easy for his mind to travel down this pathway even when there was no legitimate need for the worry.

I encouraged Brett to attend one of our programs and, once he realised that the worrying was a habit that could be broken, he felt like there was light at the end of the tunnel. He made a commitment to use neuroplasticity as his friend, not his enemy. Every time he noticed the habit of worry taking over his thoughts, he directed his attention instead to the positive aspects of his life. It was hard at first. But as new pathways developed, he found that it became easier and he no longer experienced daily worry.

^ ^ ^ ^ ^

› brain basics

You don't need to be a neuroscientist to understand your brain. A few simple facts can make the world of difference and completely change your view on what is and what is not within your control.

‹ important brain fact 1: *your brain changes itself*

› Your brain is made up of 100 billion neurons or nerve cells. These neurons are like trees with branches reaching out in many directions. Learning happens when neurons connect with each other and form a pathway through which electrical signals flow. Consider this simple example of teaching a child not to touch a hot cup of tea. As the child reaches out and you raise your voice to say 'no, that's hot!', electrical signals flow through the set of neurons that associate touching the cup with danger. These signals form a connection between the neurons that is strengthened through repetition. The more times that signals flow between these sets of neurons, the more strongly wired the learning becomes, until the growing child no longer needs the reinforcement to avoid this danger.

This is how your view of the world is formed. Your brain associates things with each other, and forms increasingly complex sets of neural connections to describe the world as you believe it to be.

Every day you are essentially doing one of three things:

› one You **reinforce what you have already learnt** by sticking with your view of the world, strengthening existing neural connections eg. cleaning your teeth the same way every day.

› two You **learn something new** and form new connections between different neurons eg. someone takes you to a new coffee shop you had previously only driven past and you find it has a courtyard out the back. The experience forms additional neural connections to the ones you had from just driving past, and now you have a more complete view of the place. You have learnt something.

› three You **find that something you believed is no longer the case**, and the connections between neurons that created the previous learning are weakened eg. seeing someone you thought was not very nice do a Good Samaritan act challenges your view of this person and you have to 'unlearn' part of your previous view to accommodate this new perspective. Signals run down different neural pathways and, because the existing ones do not receive their normal reinforcement, the connections are weakened.

Your brain remains 'plastic' throughout life and is able to learn and unlearn in this same way at any stage. However the process becomes harder with age, because the connections you have already made create default pathways or 'ruts' along which the electrical signals prefer to flow. Just as water trickling down a mountain flows more easily along worn grooves, your brain is designed to choose the pathway that requires the least energy. So when you are challenged to learn something new or change your view, this requires more energy in the form of increased levels of attention and effort. So learning can become more difficult as you age.

Many studies have shown that when you use your brain in a certain way, permanent changes are made to its structure. In fact it's similar to physical exercise. If you train your body, your muscles grow. If you train your mind, the responding areas of the brain will grow. Take the example of London cabbies. Prospective cab drivers must spend two years learning London geography before being granted a licence. A study found that the part of their brain associated with spatial memory became enlarged through this process, and the more seasoned cabbies revealed especially prominent growth. The brains of musicians are also different to non-musicians, with studies of pianists showing modifications in their auditory cortex.[2] These studies tell us that repeated patterns start taking over more cortical real estate. This explains why habits become so much easier and natural over time. The brain's structure will change, based on how you use it.

‹ the way you see the world

› The building of neural pathways explains why it is possible for different people to have a different perspective on the same thing. A child raised on a farm may love the smell of animals in the barn and know exactly how to milk a cow. A city child may rear back in disgust at the same smell, and experience fear when finding themselves too close to a large cow. Alternatively, the city child may be comfortable in crowds and know exactly how to navigate through the supermarket checkout and the busy carpark at the local shopping centre. In the same situation, the country child may find this as overwhelming as a visit to a foreign country.

Each child's behavior is a reflection of the different neural connections that have been formed and reinforced in their unique brains. Neither is worse or better, just different. We all have pathways in our brain that have become 'ruts'. They are often mindsets or habits of mind that we have developed without really being aware of them. Some of these pathways are helpful shortcuts that make your life easier, such as knowing how to turn on your computer and find your files. But some of them create limiting mindsets that cloud your outlook, your actions, and therefore your results, eg. checking your email every few minutes even when you know there is unlikely to be anything important there. Your brain does not distinguish between what is good for it and what is harmful. Just as your body can develop a bad habit that is hard to change eg. biting fingernails, the brain adopts whichever habit you focus on. It is just as easy to become very well-practised at being negative as it is to become well-practised at being positive.

‹ change your mind

› When you think about changing your life, you probably say to yourself 'I've got to stop *doing* that and starting *doing* this.' We naturally focus on actions and behaviours because that is what we can see.

∨　∨　∨　∨　∨

› The first thing Jodie wanted to talk about, when we caught up after the school reunion, was her problems at work. She was very keen to get better at delegating work to others. She realised that rather than getting her staff to take over some of the regular work she had always done, she was still taking a lot of it home each night. This didn't fit well now that she was a mum. She set herself a goal over the coming fortnight to pass specific tasks to her staff. But the next time I saw her she admitted she'd failed dismally. 'The deadlines were so tight, I just knew it was quicker to do it myself. There's no time to do it differently!'

Although Jodie found it time-consuming to do all the work, at least she felt in control when she did it herself. Whenever she tried to delegate the work, she actually became quite stressed because she was not sure the work would be delivered on time. And this stress caused her to hesitate, slip back into her comfort zone, and do the work herself. The solution for Jodie lay not in trying harder to delegate, but in recognising the habit of mind that had become a rut.

∧　∧　∧　∧　∧

The diagram below reveals how many steps occur between a thought and an action, and these steps all happen in the blink of an eye. In Jodie's case her initial thought when she brought the option of delegating work to mind was *But will they do it the way I usually do it ...?* This thought was connected to a complex set of neurons that had developed over many years in Jodie's brain that told her 'the way I do this is the best and fastest way' and this triggered a mindset 'the work won't get done in time and I won't be able to deliver to my boss.'

In Jodie's brain, as in all our brains, chemicals are constantly being brewed and wait expectantly for the brain to send them off to the four corners of our body. Like tiny messengers, these chemicals tell the cells in the body to act: fight or flight; laugh or cry; demand or plead; rest or wake. Jodie's brain, sensing the threat of not meeting a deadline, triggered her fear of losing control. Stress chemicals flooded her body and she reverted to her most well-known and trusted response to the situation: do it yourself.

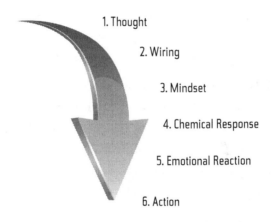

1. Thought

2. Wiring

3. Mindset

4. Chemical Response

5. Emotional Reaction

6. Action

The further down these steps that you intervene to create change, the less effective your intervention will be. It is only by examining and consciously choosing your thoughts, that you can genuinely control your feelings and your actions.

‹ i'm addicted

› You can get addicted to your own brain's chemicals, just as people get addicted to external substances they put into their body. In fact, drugs of abuse simply recruit this mechanism in the brain. When you trigger the same emotions over and over again, the brain and body start looking for this pattern, even positioning you to ensure you activate it. Any emotion can become addictive and we are all potential addicts, so it is important to carefully choose your habits. Angry people seem to constantly find themselves in situations that trigger anger. Happy people seem to more often find themselves in happy situations. This is not an accident or just life circumstances.

‹ thinking is the same as doing

› Thoughts hold as much power as actions when it comes to laying down the pathways in your brain. If you have angry thoughts but somehow suppress them, you are still laying down the wiring that will make the habit difficult to change. The power of thoughts was demonstrated in an interesting experiment at the Harvard Medical School and led by neuroscientist Alvaro Pascual-Leone, where participants were required to learn and practise a small five-finger piano exercise. The participants of one group were instructed to play as fluidly as they could, trying to keep to the metronome's 60 beats per minute. Every day for five days, the volunteers practised for two hours. At the end of each practice session, they did a Transcranial Magnetic Stimulation (TMS) test that allowed scientists to infer the function of neurons. The finding was consistent with a number of other studies at the time, showing that the more you use a particular area of the brain, the more it grows.

Pascual-Leone then went a step further by having another group of participants merely think about practising the piano exercise. They played the piece of music in their mind, while holding their hands still and simply imagining how they would move their fingers. When the scientists compared the TMS data on the group who played the piano versus the group who imagined it, they revealed that thinking about something also alters the physical structure and function of your brain. The TMS revealed that the region of the motor cortex that controls the fingers also grew larger in the group who only imagined playing the music.[3] This study reinforces that it's what's going on inside your head that's most important. Followed through with action or not, you still lay down pathways that reinforce your thinking.

Jodie finally recognised the rut she had been falling into and that she was being a control freak. By embracing a new mindset, 'my role as a leader is to build the skills of others', delegating tasks to her staff eventually became an action that gave her pleasure as she helped staff to learn something new, rather than a stressful action that triggered her threat response.

It is important to get to know your brain, monitor your thoughts, and see which of your mindsets are helping or hindering you. Neuroplasticity means that even though you have created ruts or mindsets in your life so far, your brain remains plastic and you can 'change your mind' and start creating the life you want.

‹ important brain fact 2: your brain is very sociable

› Nothing in the world evolves without a purpose. The forces of nature over time are such that any attribute profitable to the survival of a species is retained and strengthened. Anything that is of no value fades and dies out. This very simple principle of the evolutionary world explains much about our human brain, because your brain is your most crucial survival tool. It is the place that receives and interprets all the messages from your sight, hearing, taste, smell and touch. It determines if something or someone is friend or foe, danger or advantage.

The greatest leap of human brain development was the one that enabled our complex communication with each other. Collaboration of the type that took humans from nomadic family groups to larger settled tribes is truly the source of our modern day life and distinguishes us from every other animal. If that fledgling communication ability had repeatedly led to conflict and death, you can be sure that early humans would have evolved into a totally different creature. Solitude would have been rewarded and we'd be more like tigers or bears than the social creatures we are today.

But instead we were rewarded for belonging to a group, for contributing as part of a community, and for being in harmony with others. And because what the brain practises gets stronger, this ability to live in community with others is one of the most strongly wired abilities of our brain.

While it is easy to think the brain is a well-developed analysis machine, our focus on facts, figures and data are more recent uses of the brain. Well before we relied on these decision-making tools, we were listening, empathising and interpreting the intentions of others.

The social brain knows what others are trying to communicate, what their intentions are, and what emotion they are experiencing, and it does not need a shared language to achieve this. Groundbreaking research by Paul Ekman in the 1960s revealed that emotions, previously believed to be culturally determined, are in fact biological and shared across human cultures. His research with remote tribes in Papua New Guinea found that members of this tribe could reliably identify emotions on the faces of those from cultures to which they had never been exposed. They could also ascribe facial expressions when a situation was described.[4] The expression of emotion is our shared language.

Do you ever get an instinct about someone when you first meet them? You immediately know whether you can trust them or not. And you don't have a rational reason for it.

George is a successful businessman about town and he once told us he uses what he calls the three-second rule. When meeting someone new, he shakes their hand and waits for three seconds to see how he feels about them. He swears by this technique and says it has never let him down.

While it may seem a bit like sorcery, in fact your well-honed social brain is picking up signals, even though you would struggle to explain them logically. But remember, in our early days in tribes it was a matter of pure survival to be able to assess someone on approach.

‹ mirrors and viruses, pain and stories

› It is thought that our capacity for empathy and our incredibly well-honed human radar can be explained by a set of neurons in our brain called 'mirror' neurons. Have you ever watched a movie and found yourself experiencing the sadness of the character? It's possible to get so emotionally involved in a movie, it feels like the story is actually happening to you! Or maybe you've watched a football game and your muscles were twitching as if you were actually on the field playing the ball. In both situations your mirror neurons are active and causing these emotional and physical responses. Their job is to make you feel as if you are living in the other person's mind and experiencing their thoughts and emotions. It explains how it is possible to learn by simply watching others perform a task. But it also has the effect of causing actions and emotions to move through a crowd like a virus. Just sit at any café and watch the people around you. If someone pulls out their mobile phone to check messages, you will undoubtedly see another person follow suit very soon after. It's the new virus but we can't blame the phones! It's our own brains doing what they have been trained to do over millions of years.

The social brain explains some other game-changing things that start to make sense of the way life can unfold. Scientists have found that the brain registers social pain in exactly the same way that it registers physical pain. If you are excluded by others in a social situation, your brain would register that slight in the same way as if you had been physically hurt. So being excluded really *is* like a slap in the face! The brain simply does not know the difference between the two experiences.

˅   ˅   ˅   ˅   ˅

› Lately Sarah had been feeling 'on the outer' and the school reunion had just reinforced it. Many of her long time friends now had babies and Sarah often felt left out of conversations and group gatherings. She was surprised how strongly she had reacted to this. It had undermined her confidence and she had retreated even more. She often felt sad and noticed that her mood was starting to rub off on those around her. Her partner thought she was acting like a teenager. Sometimes she felt like she was going crazy and overreacting.

Had Sarah understood this simple principle about the social brain, she would have recognised her reaction and felt more able to handle it. Had her partner understood it, he may have been a bit more sympathetic and nursed her through the pain, just as he would if she'd been physically injured and was hobbling around on a pair of crutches. And her friends would be horrified to think that their actions felt the same to Sarah as if they had all slapped her. But without this simple knowledge of the brain, we are easily hobbled and our world is unnecessarily full of the walking wounded.

˄   ˄   ˄   ˄   ˄

The social brain also provides an explanation for many other things that we know from experience to be true. Stories light up your brain in ways that facts and figures just cannot do. So too does purpose and meaning, in ways that goals and milestones fail to achieve. At heart we are still tribal members around the campfire, learning from the stories of others and driven by the need to belong. Don't underestimate the refined nature of your social brain and its ability to affect the way you think and act.

‹ important brain fact 3: *your brain is easily scared*

› Most of what drives your behavior is governed by the principle that your brain is a survival tool. And the way that it has found to be most effective at guaranteeing your survival is through the threat and reward mechanism. Put simply, your brain will cause you to move away from threats and move towards rewards. Imagine you are walking along a dark forest path and you notice something in the distance shaped in a coil. Your brain will send out chemicals to trigger your flight response, before you've even had time to determine if this really is a snake or just a coil of tree debris. It is only after a few moments of heightened attention and examination that you can overcome this automatic response and calm your brain down with the information that all is well and the threat is not real.

Along with other animals, we share this automatic response through a part of the brain called the amygdala. The threat response is not only triggered by situations of physical survival. We now live in a time when threat is interpreted in social situations, work situations and our general environment.

As a survival mechanism, your brain is more highly attuned to threat than it is to reward. While it wants to move towards reward, it gives more attention to threat. It's only logical that we would have evolved to examine a threat closely and not turn away from it until we are sure it is not going to cause us danger. On the other hand, we experience a short period of satisfaction from reward, then we move on. No wonder lasting happiness seems so elusive!

But because neuroplasticity means that what you focus on grows, it can be very easy to slip from a normal state of threat alert to one of threat obsession. Have you ever noticed that your daily TV news and newspapers are filled with bad news and potential threats? Your brain tells you to pay attention and check if there are dangers that can directly affect you. And this threat alert will also tell you to keep watching, and come back again tomorrow and the next day ...

The habit of noticing threat more obviously than reward means that we often give more energy to the very things we wish to avoid, rather than cultivating the pleasant things that we would like to grow. It can make you give up your dreams, rather than take a chance on something that appears risky. It can hold you back from the perfect opportunity. It can make you assume the worst case scenario is the most likely.

ⅴ   ⅴ   ⅴ   ⅴ   ⅴ

› At the school reunion, Bill told us a story from early in his career when he was a senior policy adviser with the government. He was leaving for home one night after putting in a 12-hour day. His manager caught him on the way out, asking him to come to her office early the next morning. Bill spent the rest of the night sweating on it, because he had recently thrown his hat into the ring for a promotion and he was really suspicious they weren't going to give him a fair run. All night he went over different ways that the conversation could go, and it was all very negative.

By the next morning he had worked himself into a state. When he walked into his manager's office his heart was beating fast. She started to tell him that he had not been given the promotion and Bill got very defensive, bringing up every situation where he felt he hadn't been supported. His boss told him to settle down. The reason he hadn't got the promotion was that there was a more important role that they thought Bill was ready for, if he wanted to give it a go. It was definitely the prize role in the area and Bill had always wanted it. He felt very stupid and wondered how it had unravelled so badly.

Bill's hyper-vigilant amygdala sensed a threat when his boss requested a meeting with him. His brain quickly began formulating ways to deal with the threat—and fast! By the time he had stewed over and over his threat story, he was convinced that he was going to be treated unfairly. As soon as he heard something that sounded threatening, his brain released the chemicals that moved him into fight mode. He was still embarrassed about his reaction years later, and was just grateful that they still gave him a chance.

^ ^ ^ ^ ^

› the five fears

Your brain's threat response is as old as the human race. Because it evolved to deal with a life so different to that which many of us face today, you could almost call it outdated. As your survival tool, it still does a number of things that made a lot of sense in the lives of our ancestors. But the unfortunate side effect is that many of these default threat responses hinder your efforts to thrive. Now your brain searches not just for direct threats to your physical safety, but it is alerted by many common experiences that have been linked over time to your physical survival.

Consider these common fears that are triggered by the brain's threat response to perceived threats deeply wired in the human brain.

Common Threats	The Five Fears
The threat of making a mistake—leaves you at risk of becoming vulnerable, weakened or rejected	Fear of Failure
The threat of the unknown—leaves you at risk of being unable to survive when conditions change	Fear of Losing Control
The threat of rejection—leaves you at risk of being left to fend for yourself and being denied the benefit of safety in numbers	Fear of Standing Out
The threat of scarcity—leaves you at risk of not having enough resources to survive	Fear of Missing Out
The threat of being held responsible—leaves you at risk of being rejected or becoming vulnerable	Fear of Facing the Truth

While you may not identify with all of these fears and you may not feel like they dominate your life, they have a way of influencing your actions in very subtle ways. For example, I'm not a control freak but I know that my fear of losing control stopped me recently from attending a friend's party. She wanted to do something different and arranged for us all to jump on a bus that would take us on a mystery tour to many exciting destinations. No expense was spared and I have no doubt she would have done a magnificent job organising the day. But all I could think was *I won't be able to come home in my own time. Will there be bugs, will I get sunburned, will I have to do something embarrassing? If there are winding roads I'll get travel sickness ...* And of course I convinced myself not to go. I came up with a nice excuse and no-one was surprised. They know this is not my sort of thing.

But they are too polite to point out I'm just threatened by the thought of losing control!

These common threats and fears are not the only mindsets that can stand in your way. We each have our own wiring created over our lifetime. These assumptions, attitudes, expectations, habits and preferences can combine to hold you back, so understanding your own mind is crucial.

› you're a mind gardener

You're a mind gardener. This is so important we are going to say it again. **You are a mind gardener.** Every moment of every day you cultivate your mind whether you realise it or not. There is no moment in your life, since the day you were born, that you have not been a mind gardener. We're not saying that you are a mind gardener if you like this book or decide to try some of the ideas we suggest. We're saying that even if you don't want to be one, you are. Because it is your every thought, action and experience that wires, shapes, moulds and refines your brain and shapes your life.

That's pretty significant. Because every part of your life is determined by your brain. And you can choose to let it happen in the generally unconscious way that many of us bumble through life, or you can wake up, get conscious, and design your mind garden. But either way you are, and will always be, a mind gardener.

‹ the unconscious mind gardener

› Let's face it, most of us are on autopilot most of the time, for most of our lives. And for most of life's experiences, you probably get away with it. We're not saying that every little activity you do requires conscious reflection and choice. Your brain is designed so you don't have to do this. It learns routine activities and allows you to repeat them so you don't have to waste vital energy relearning something you've already done before. The sequence of movements when you clean your teeth can be repeated blindfolded. But let's flip this on its head. Every time you do an action on autopilot, you train your brain to **not** pay attention. This is the silent deadly trick of the brain that goes unnoticed. That everything you do, intentional or not, can become a habit for your brain.

Your husband, wife, mother, father, daughter, son, best friend, boss, colleague, bus driver, shop owner ... every one of them is mind gardening right now. It's easy to say 'well, I can see that I'm a mind gardener when I do a yoga class or read a book'. But here's the rub. You probably do more to cultivate the habits in your mind the moment you leave the yoga class or put down the book. Because your brain continues to absorb your experiences, play with your thoughts, slip into habitual mindsets, judge, criticise, ruminate and chatter. And when this activity of mind continues in the background untended, the garden of your mind grows.

What you give attention to grows. Your attention is the sun and the rain showering down on the plants in your mind garden. A thought dropped into your mind by a stranger's comment is a seed that becomes nothing without your own attention dwelling on the thought and encouraging it to take root.

∨　∨　∨　∨　∨

> Amanda has long had a habit of interpreting every situation in her life as negative. From the driver in front who does not move over quickly enough, to the smell of the neighbour's BBQ floating up to her balcony, it is like her brain zeros in only on the information in that situation that can be turned into a 'bad' story.

A weed had propagated over many years in her brain. Her mother had the same pattern, and being exposed to her viewpoint and reactions to the world during her formative years had wired Amanda similarly. The weed does not need much more than the occasional watering now and then. It is like a strangler vine, squeezing the life out of any rising flowers or saplings of happiness, and making it impossible to see positive and happy situations that really do exist around her.

^ ^ ^ ^ ^

Weeds are hardy plants and the negative thoughts in your mind have this characteristic. They are clever at sourcing the nutrients they need in your brain and have developed long and far-reaching root systems. This enables them to sprout far and wide and appear in unexpected places. How often have people who struggle with weight loss found that the weight has fallen off not through diet, but because they have finally addressed a weed that took root in their mind many years ago?

While weeds find their place and grow well when the garden is most ignored, it seems that the positive and happy plants that we would prefer to grow in our mind are much more vulnerable and require more active tending and cultivation. This is because of the brain's prioritisation of threat over reward. It is important to remember the challenge that this presents, because when your threat response is triggered, fears are likely to rise up and steer you off the path of the well-lived life without you even noticing.

‹ what's your garden like?

› What would someone proclaim when they first see your mind garden? Would they see fields of happy thoughts that have taken root and propagated kindness, love, gratitude and cheer? Or would they find creeping vines of worry, stress, and anxiety intertwined with negativity? Maybe they would find open fields with diverse pockets of curiosity, adventure, creativity and wonder; or orderly rows of logic with repeated patterns of sensibility.

Now that you understand the very basics of the brain and its wiring, let's delve more deeply into some of the common obstacles on life's journey. We will explore the five fears that have their origins in primitive times, when the ability to sense threats was a survival imperative. You may identify with one of them strongly or perhaps relate to an element in a few of them. Although they are labelled 'fears' you may not relate to them as something you are consciously afraid of. But rest assured they will be at play somewhere in your behaviour. You may also have some unique mindsets that will come to light as you read this book. Either way it's time to conquer the fears that are holding you back from a life well lived. And the first step is to understand them a little bit more.

> the fear of failure: it's time to take a chance

> the failure club

Oprah Winfrey is the world's most successful talk show host. For decades she ran the highest rated program of its kind. She is indisputably a successful person, maybe the most influential woman in the world in her time. And she has always been successful, right?

Richard Branson is a brilliant business magnate, best known for his Virgin Group of over 400 companies. His wealth is in the billions and he is used as the shining example of how to create great businesses. He is clearly very successful. And he's always excelled at everything, right?

Michael Jordan is one of the greatest basketball players of all time. He has held the NBA record for highest career regular season scoring average. His individual accolades are too many to name and young people strive to emulate his success. And he has always been a winner, right?

Wrong, wrong and wrong! Every single one of these people has failed. In fact, they have failed over and over again. And that's what has made them a success.

Oprah lost her first job out of college as a co-anchor of the six o'clock news after eight months. She faced criticism that she was too emotional and did not have the right hair. Richard Branson was a college dropout and has many failed business ideas in his closet. Michael Jordan was cut from his high school basketball team because his coach didn't think he had enough skill. Look at any successful person and you'll see someone who has failed, and failed often. But you'll also see someone who knows how to bounce back. Taking a chance and embracing failure are prerequisites to success.

It's hard to imagine your favourite successful people as anything other than the confident and accomplished people you see before you today. But successful people often joke that it takes ten years of hard work to become an overnight success. And during that time they have worn many other labels as they made false starts, changed direction, experimented, learnt great lessons and experienced many, many failures.

Fear of failure is probably the most common and crippling mindset that can prevent people from achieving success. And because it is a side effect of some of the brain's natural mechanisms, you find it universally—in all fields, ages and lifestyles. Fear of failure is seen in artists who never finish their piece of work, because they don't believe it will ever be perfect. Business people put off important decisions, waiting for more information and the perfect conditions that never actually come. Partners stay in unsatisfying relationships because they fear they have missed the boat and are too old to start again on the road to love. Young children avoid trying something new, in case they get it wrong and bring disappointment to the eyes of their parents.

It seems like 'fear of failure' is a club that the people around you have secretly joined, and the first time they declare their membership is when you share your intention to act on your dreams. That's when they try to recruit you to the club. I come from a family where my parents and siblings have worked in safe and traditional fields of endeavour, generally employed by others. When I announced my intention to venture into my own business I experienced very subdued responses. 'You know that 80 per cent of small businesses don't survive the first two years.' 'Your career was going so well.' 'Why don't you stay a few more years and take your long service leave'. 'You'll need at least three months of living expenses up your sleeve as a buffer.' As a result, I structured my whole life to reduce risks when I started my first business. I rented out my home and moved in with a friend, delayed some desired purchases of new season clothes and swapped to public transport. The 'fear of failure' club had successfully recruited me and, even though they had not halted my decision, they had significantly affected the mindsets and behaviours I adopted, as I ventured into my dream. Many years later, I think my family still fear for my security, often asking 'how's business?' Their fear is not simply for me, it is a reflection of a mindset that shaped their lives long before I was even born.

Fear of failure is a great big obstacle on the road to success. However it is a fear that can be overcome and even turned to your advantage. It's time to resign from the 'fear of failure' club and join the 'failure' club!

› you used to love failing

There's got to be a good explanation for why someone would fear failure more than they would fear that they might never realise their dreams. Because it isn't logical to shy away from the very thing that lights you up and gives meaning to your life. So how did humans become so illogical?

Failing was your first success strategy in life. In your first few years you learnt more than you ever would again in such a short space of time. You learnt to walk by falling, eat by missing your mouth and speak by jumbling up your words! And when you made these mistakes you would have been greeted with the smiling face and clapping hands of the people around you, giving you all the encouragement you needed to try again. You felt safe and your failures were celebrated.

Then a few years later, you were taught that failing is to be avoided. School systems do not tend to celebrate failure and, while transformation is taking place in pockets around the world, many adults would have tasted childhood failure with the sour flavours of embarrassment and shame. You are one of the lucky ones if you made it through your school years without being wired up with the fear of failure, techniques for avoiding failure, and strategies to hide your failures. Most of us learn at a very early age to start avoiding things that put us at risk of failing.

I still vividly recall the time in Grade Five when we got our school results back for the term. The teacher thought it was a good idea to rearrange our classroom so that we were all in a line, from the smartest kids up the front through to the poor performing kids at the back. Our brains are designed to get better at whatever we reinforce, whether good or bad. The kids at the back were not only humiliated by the label, they started to live up to it. They thought they didn't have any other option but to fail, not as a way to learn better for next time but simply as an end in itself. And there was no joy for the kids up the front either, concerned about maintaining their position in the line. Their grades suffered too as they took less risks in case they failed, and over time their grades matched this fear.

And this failure dialogue continues through high school and college. Pass or fail. Dux or dunce. Get good grades and you'll be a success in life. Get poor ones and you'll end up on the scrap heap. It's no longer safe to fail.

By the time you get a job and a chance to break free, you realise organisations are just the same. They focus on why something didn't work and who's accountable. You learn not to stick your neck out, question superiors, or go outside the policy. 'That's the way we do things around here' is a common mantra that halts creativity and experimentation in its tracks. Because if we do it differently, it might fail.

We see this fear rear its head time and time again, when we run our *Conscious Leadership* programs in organisations. One of the more obvious examples occurred when we ran two consecutive programs with a new client. The first group of leaders to undertake the program was made up of people recently appointed to their first leadership role. They were blank canvases, thirsty for skills and knowledge. They gave 120 per cent and the results they achieved were truly remarkable.

We expected the second group to be similar, but they couldn't have been more different. For the first two days of the program they hardly uttered a word. Frequent open questions to the group were met with silence. The explanation by some participants following subtle enquiry was 'Oh, we already know all this stuff'. But the way they glanced fearfully at visiting senior managers told us what was really going on. They had a fear of failure. Answering questions and speaking in front of the group held huge risks for them. After all, what if they didn't get it right?

Why did this second group hold a fear that was not displayed by the first group? We found out that this group was made up of managers who were more senior than the first group and who had been in their management roles for longer. Some were even the managers of those in the first program. Clearly in this organisation, as in many, management progression was accompanied by the expectation you would have all the right answers, never make mistakes and always look like you knew everything. The group progressed little until we were able to have an open and honest discussion about how the fear of failure arises, why learning to fail is one of the keys to success, and how to embrace the fear of failure. It was only when they took a chance and dared to fail that they began to flourish.

When you were little, you used to love failing. But then you were expected to 'grow up' and start getting things right all the time. The luxury of a second chance faded, even though progress is rarely achieved without experimentation, learning and trying again. But maybe there is another explanation for why we are so hard on ourselves and others, and why the fear of failure is a common trap to achieving success.

› failure is a threat

Your brain's threat/reward system is a major driver of your behaviour. This neurological mechanism evolved as a necessity for survival, motivating you to take note of potential threats and respond quickly when they loom. Your distant ancestors lived in a world that required them to be alert to a whole range of physical threats or face dire consequences. There was rarely a second chance if cornered by a sabre-toothed tiger! They became wired to look for threats, recognise them, examine them to check if they were dangerous, and watch them until they moved out of the danger zone. And they had only two choices on how to respond in the face of threat: meet it head on and fight, or turn on their heels and run. In the situations faced by your ancestors, failure did not just mean embarrassment, it more often meant death. So fear of threats and the possible consequences is a highly-evolved strategy that has served the human race well.

Your brain still functions the same way as did that of your early ancestors. You are a threat scanner, a threat avoider and a threat fighter. But the shape of the threats that face you in the modern world are very different. Failing at a job can be processed as a threat to status. Failing at a marriage can be processed as a threat to belonging. Failing at education can be processed as a threat to security. And the threat response does not wait to see if these consequences materialise. The threat response is activated as soon as your mind starts visualising them.

Concern about how you are perceived by others goes hand in hand with fear of failure. We saw this first hand when we were working with Ruby. Even though she was a dynamic person, it was impossible to miss the sadness in her voice. It was only when we travelled together for work that we got an insight into her personal life. She had a deeply dissatisfying marriage. She was at the point where she and her husband rarely spoke unless it was to plan their week's logistics. There was no love, care, or even interest in each other. In fact, they were starting to drag each other down through emotional abuse. But she wouldn't contemplate getting out of it. That would be failing. More alarmingly, she would not consider counselling or even buying a self-help book. Because that, too, would look like she had failed.

It seems crazy that the perception of other people would be more important than the happiness in your own life, but research shows that your brain's threat response kicks in when you think you might compare unfavourably to someone else.[5] Your brain does not distinguish a threat to status as being different from a threat to your life. This seems a huge leap, but maybe it isn't. Several studies have suggested that we are biologically programmed to be concerned about our status because it is linked to our survival. High status is related to longevity and health. In Sir Michael Marmot's studies he found that people with PhDs live longer than those with Masters degrees, those with a Masters live longer than those with an undergraduate degree, and those with any degree live longer than those who left school early. Similarly, actors who have won an Oscar will live, on average, three years longer than those who were nominated for the award but missed out.[6]

This implies that success is not something we assess against our own internal radar, but something we assess in comparison to others. Your brain's defence mechanism is not activated by the thought of not achieving your own dreams, but it lights up immediately when it appears you might fall short in relation to others.

› failing to achieve

It's not failure that hinders you, it's the fear itself. In a state of fear, your actions are not at their best. The moment your mind adopts a fear mindset, your body quickly moves into the fight or flight mode. So you are either going to challenge the cause of your fear, or move away from it. Neither of these sound like the actions of successful people. Imagine if Michael Jordan 'moved away from' basketball because he did not want to feel the sting of failure again. He may have succeeded in something else, but more likely he would have repeated this pattern of moving away from other risks, criticisms or doubts. Imagine if Oprah had 'challenged' the opinion of her bosses and, instead of accepting a different role they offered her and completing her contract, had fought for a contract payout and moved on to another field of endeavour. She may never have stumbled into the role that was her perfect fit, and she might never have learnt one of the lessons that she shares generously with others: to have faith in where life is taking you.

The threat state triggered by the fear of failure blinds you, not just metaphorically, but literally. As the body diverts resources such as glucose and oxygen in preparation for fight or flight, it withdraws activity in non-essential areas of the brain and the body. Your attention is heightened, but is focused directly on the threat. You brain literally blocks out information that it determines to be irrelevant to the threat at hand. Exposure to stressful situations causes increased activity in the amygdala (associated with fear and anxiety), causing this area of the brain to literally grow. At the same time, neurons shrink and lose their connections in the prefrontal cortex, the executive area of the brain where conscious decisions are made.[7] This results in a loss of brain flexibility, critical analysis, creativity and decision-making. So when you are experiencing the fear of failure, you simply do not have the full resources of your powerful brain at your disposal. You operate instead in a state of autopilot, and your choices will be compromised.

To be successful where others are not, you must be able to see things that others don't even notice, and act where others would hesitate. You must be prepared to experiment with the untested, swallow the shame of falling short when compared to others, and be willing to try again when something does not work. Cultivating a mindset that says 'take a chance' will set you free from the perceived pain of failure, and change your path through life.

› failing to learn

Our friend has just discovered that he loves to cook. An intuitive type, he picks up ideas everywhere. On a recent visit to a French restaurant, he saw an entrée that had him transfixed, and he decided to try it at home. The challenge rested in how to deep fry a whole egg while still maintaining a runny yellow yolk. Unable to track down any useful information on the internet, he simply chose a starting point and gave it a go. Three days later with ten test eggs in the bin, he finally found the right combination of boiling time and deep frying time for the egg and a marvellous meal was made. It would have been much easier to doubt his ability, give up after the second egg, and eventually put it out of his mind. But by taking a chance, every collapsed egg offered a lesson that took him closer to success, the journey became fun, and it ended well.

But you don't have to achieve the original goal, for something to be labelled a success. In 2010 we embarked on a publicity program aimed at securing a place on a TV show watched by millions of people worldwide. We created a campaign in which we broadcast weekly movies on You Tube, made audacious offers, and sent messages through our network that were designed to challenge thinking. We took risks we had never done before and we got noticed! Then the TV show aired, but we weren't on it. Failure or success?

This was perceived two ways. Many well-meaning colleagues expressed their sympathy 'Oh we're really sorry you didn't get on. And after all that hard work too.' They focused on our failure. But we saw it in a totally different light. Our final You Tube movie was a tribute to everything we had learnt and a 'thank you' to all the people who had helped us. And to this day, people still comment on how inspiring they found that last movie. For us, the destination itself was actually irrelevant. It had acted only as a motivator for a journey of learning. It was the most successful campaign so far in our decade in business. We quadrupled our social media following, we appeared in various media, and we made some great contacts who still promote us for free today. We learnt how to make our own movies, got a presence on You Tube and, most importantly, confronted some personal mindsets that needed to change. What part of this could be called a failure? Would we do it again? You bet. But we'll do an even better job next time, because of the learnings along the way. And this is how success unfolds.

Failure in life is inevitable. You did it when you were a baby, and even if you've become an expert at avoiding it now, it's time to accept that you *have* failed many times in your life. And you did bounce back. Without realising it, you actually do have the skills to experience failure and learn from it, and you do have the courage to bounce back and move on. Your brain is only trying to protect you, when it switches on the alarm bells designed to pull you back to the pack where it is safe. Understanding this default response can empower you to set it aside and take a chance.

› failing to grow

Fear of failure equals failure to grow. The saying 'you can learn from your mistakes' is more than just a cliché. Psychologists from the University of Exeter[8] discovered that you learn a lot more when your predictions are incorrect than when they are correct. Your brain reacts in just 0.1 seconds when it sees something that has caused you to make a mistake in the past. Unless you've tried and made a mistake, how can you build this early warning system? Instinct for the right decisions seems to be a characteristic of successful people, but they build this strength by making mistakes.

Learning and growth is at its peak when you are out of your comfort zone. Consider the greatest personal growth periods in your life. They often occur in the wake of a personal crisis, like relationship break down, job loss, natural disaster or the unexpected loss of a loved one. But the growth only occurs when you face the crisis and move forward. Research also suggests that those who believe they will grow from such experiences are more likely to bounce back and make fewer errors in the future.[9]

Personal growth also accompanies the great events that are common throughout life, such as moving to a new city or country, starting a family, or retirement. Interestingly, but not surprisingly in light of our growing understanding of the brain, it is during such times that you experience a boost in the growth of new neurons. You will never come through significant events, whether positive or negative, without a brain that is different to the one you had before it happened.

Failing teaches a whole range of skills that are important for life. That's probably why it's one of the first strategies you adopted as a baby. It teaches patience: that you don't always get what you want when you want it, and that sometimes you need to wait. It teaches perseverance and motivation: that you can achieve anything, if you are prepared to try and try again. And it teaches self-reflection and problem-solving: that you can improve, if you are prepared to learn from the past and incorporate these learnings into your future actions.

› fearing the fear

People who live their lives well can distinguish between what they need to keep doing consistently over time, and what they need to do differently. If you have a fear of failure, you naturally resist the thought that you need to do something different. You don't give yourself the chance to fail and learn, because you won't even line up at the starting line. In the meantime, the person who operates with the mindset of embracing failure, jumps before the starter's gun and gives their all. It does not mean they did not feel fear, they just recognised it for what it was and did not let it drive their actions. Only two outcomes are possible for them: they'll get it right and succeed, or they'll get it wrong, learn from it and try again. They succeed, if not at the original goal, then at something new they found along the way. Truly, the person who takes a chance cannot fail.

There are many people who have stayed in the same job for 20 years because they are too scared to try something new. They convince themselves they have 20 years' experience when, in reality, they have one year of experience duplicated 20 times. Yes, they have felt safe; but all too often they also feel unfulfilled and that they have missed out on something important.

v v v v v

› When I met with Brett just a few weeks after the school reunion, he updated me on his life. He had bought a beautiful house in a great suburb, and was happy with his loving wife and sweet children. But, for the last 15 years, he had been feeling a gnawing emptiness. He couldn't remember the last time he had a fire in his belly at work, and countless job changes, promotions and relocations had done little to fix the situation. Despite the great pay cheque, he got little satisfaction from his work. His real passion lay in helping young people to reach their full potential, and he often had fantastic ideas about innovative programs and initiatives that would really hit the mark. When he talked about his ideas his face lit up, people were inspired, and he was constantly encouraged by all around him 'Why don't you do something with all these great ideas?'

But Brett could never bring himself to take the step. He felt safe in the advertising world. He was well known and respected. He'd worked his way up the ladder and all signs suggested that would continue. Whenever someone seriously probed into why he didn't act on his ideas, his demeanour would change. 'That wouldn't be a real job' he'd scoff, laughing the very notion away and changing the topic. Deep down it was clear that he did not believe he could be as successful fulfilling his passion, as he was in his current role. His first concern was for all the things he believed he would lose if it did not work out. And that fear of failure continued to hold him back. While the emptiness was painful, it was a pain he had learnt to tolerate. The unknown risk of failure was a pain he could only imagine. And his threatened brain did its job well, imagining the very worst, and triggering the flight response.

^ ^ ^ ^ ^

We hear many fantastic business ideas that we know would be winners, but the person concerned is too paralysed by the fear of failure to try them. We also hear many people say 'Look how successful those people are. I had that exact idea five years ago!' And that's what happens. If you don't take a chance, someone else will. And their mindset will keep them moving forward while those with the fear of failure watch from the sidelines.

Michael Jordan put it nicely 'But I can see how some people get frozen by the fear of failure. They get it from peers or from just thinking about the possibility of negative results. They might be afraid of looking bad or being embarrassed. That's not good enough for me. I realised that if I was going to achieve anything in life I had to be aggressive. I had to get out there and go for it. I don't believe you can achieve anything by being passive. I know fear is an obstacle for some people, but it's an illusion to me. Once I'm in there, I'm not thinking about anything except what I'm trying to accomplish. Any fear is an illusion. You think something is standing in your way but nothing is really there. What is there is an opportunity to do your best and gain some success. If it turns out my best isn't good enough, then at least I'll never be able to look back and say I was too afraid to try. Failure always made me try harder the next time.'[10]

› a healthy respect for failure

Richard Branson once said that being unafraid of failure is one the most important qualities of a champion. He tried many different things in his life, failed at many and lost millions if not billions of dollars. But he never gave up and he never let these failures stop him from achieving success.

In every sport or competition, there is a winner and a loser. It feels better to be the winner, but truth be known, losing is probably more valuable. When you lose, you learn about yourself, your strengths, the gaps and how you might adapt your approach next time. It motivates you to make changes and improve. And if you can bust through the fear of failure, then it will get easier each time, as your brain learns to suspend its threat response and allow the unknown journey to continue.

We are not suggesting that you should aim to fail or put in so little effort that failing is inevitable. Those who achieve success by embracing failure see it simply as a milestone to be acknowledged, then quickly passed by. In fact if they are honest, many of these people would say they hate failing, but they respect the lessons it offers and are not scared to hear its messages. Those who fear failure don't want to hear the messages. They try to bypass these important milestones in the mistaken belief that the journey to success can be travelled on a bed of roses.

Not only can the fear of failure prevent you from making genuine efforts to achieve your dream, it can prevent you from enjoying the pleasure of actually achieving it. Jonny Wilkinson[11], the English rugby union player, became England's hero during the 2003 Rugby World Cup, when he kicked the winning drop goal, and he is often referred to as one of the world's best rugby union players.

Despite this, he admits that his overwhelming fear of failure stopped him achieving any satisfaction from his success. He has been quoted as saying that, within 24 hours of winning the World Cup final against Australia, he felt a powerful anticlimax. 'I did not know what it really meant to be happy. I was afflicted by a powerful fear of failure and did not know how to free myself from it.'

When he was sidelined for four years with injuries, he was forced to face this fear head on. He continued: 'I came to understand that I had been living a life in which I barely featured. I had spent my time immersed in the fear of not achieving my goals and then spent my time beating myself up about the mistakes I made along the way.' A self-proclaimed obsessive perfectionist, he realised it was ruining his life.

His story reminds us that traditional success is a tricky notion. Someone who appears successful may come sliding down the other side, surprising us all with their fallibility. Then we learn more about what's going on inside and it all makes sense. Success on the surface was no success at all. It's not enough to be a winner if all you feel is the fear of losing. It's not enough to be beautiful if all you feel is the fear of imperfection. It's not enough to be recognised for your contribution if all you feel is the fear of being ignored. While you can appear successful to others, in your honest moments alone you know the truth.

Years down the track I wonder how Albert Einstein's teacher would feel now, after telling him to quit school because 'Einstein, you will never amount to anything'! And would Ludwig Von Beethoven's music teacher feel foolish for saying 'As a composer, he is hopeless'?

We all get knock-backs in life. You will never appeal to everyone 100 per cent of the time. Don't confuse one person's opinion with total failure. Don't allow a knock-back to take you off your path. But most importantly, don't allow your own fear of failure to stop you experiencing some of the greatest opportunities of your life.

> the fear of losing control: it's time to let it go

> in control or going with the flow?

It's 15 minutes until the commencement of the inaugural conference *Investigating the Mind* in Boston in 2003. We have just overcome the initial thrill of sitting in the row behind Richard Gere and we're ready to turn our attention to the upcoming speakers. A quick read of the agenda reveals that a dialogue between neuroscientists and Buddhist monks will take us through the morning. As some of the smartest and calmest people take the stage, we are fascinated by what unfolds in front of us. The scientists are checking contents on their laptop or making notes on the papers in their hands. They are asking questions of the audiovisual people, fiddling with their microphones and moving the water around in front of them. The monks are meditating.

What a difference in approach. One group displayed the behaviours that arise from a belief that you need to be planned, scripted and in control to perform. The other group showed commitment to a belief that you simply need to be present and let go of all unnecessary thought.

Until that moment, we would both admit to being much more likely to fit the model displayed by the scientists. In fact, it would never have occurred to us that there was any other way. We ran programs for groups all the time and surely they were good because of all the effort we made to ensure everything was just as it should be. Or were we missing something? Were we actually control freaks?!?

› the truth about control freaks

We all know one. The friend who organises your social events down to the last detail, but irons out all the opportunities for spontaneous fun. The boss who wants the report to look a certain way, and doesn't listen to new ideas. The parent who has their children in every sort of after-school activity and operates the household like a military camp. We are not without affection when we use this label on the ones we love; but we also use it in frustration when we deal with someone who just can't seem to bend to make it easier for us all to fit in together.

You don't need to be a control freak to find that the need to control can trip you up on your journey through life. It's another one of our protective mechanisms, driven by a brain that is trying to help you survive. For good reason, we have developed a great capacity to make plans, follow them, and act to put things right when they go off track. It's a capability that underpins the enormous advancements that humans have been able to make in shaping the world to our liking. But you can have too much of a good thing. Like all reinforced habits of mind, when it's used repetitively it becomes a default pathway, followed even when it might not be the best approach.

People who are wired for life recognise what they can and cannot control. They direct their energy towards the things they can control, and respond to resistance by looking for alternatives, not just sticking to the path they prefer. They are able to release control, even if it does not feel particularly comfortable. And ultimately, they recognise the only thing they really do control is themselves.

Nelson Mandela has shown people all over the world that it is possible to achieve peaceful change by holding out your hand to your enemy. But the man who rose to fame after his release from Robben Island in 1990 is a very different man to the one who was incarcerated in 1963. In his youth, Nelson Mandela advocated violent resistance to the injustices he saw in his country. You can imagine this young man with a picture in his mind of how he thought things *should be*, and he was prepared to do whatever it took to make the world conform to this picture. He decided that violence was the only way to get there. In the silence of his prison, no longer in control of his own days and with time and solitude to reflect, Mandela's mind began to move. His mindset was altered by reading books, taking a fresh look at his 'enemy', and finally, by letting go. While he still believed in the same vision of justice, his mind was open to new ways to get there. 'I learnt that courage was not the absence of fear, but the triumph over it. The brave man is not he who does not feel afraid, but he who conquers that fear.' Mandela realised that all he could control was himself and his response.

If Nelson Mandela had not been able to let go of his need to control, he would never have become the leader who inspired a whole nation to change. We would probably never have heard more from this angry man, except perhaps to read a small article telling of a violent rebel cut down by troops within weeks of his release. Try as you might, you can never control the complex world around you. To believe you can is one of the biggest traps on your journey through life.

› the controlling brain

Your brain wants to be your best friend. It will do anything to ensure your survival. The earliest humans who took note of when the seasons changed, where the dangerous animals resided, and which plants helped in the healing process, increased their chances of survival. They stored food, ensured they had enough warm coverings, and moved to different locations to improve their access to water and game. By taking control of the things that were within their control, they minimised the impact of the things outside their control. Those who did not act this way did not survive. The habit of taking control was a successful survival strategy and evolved into our brain wiring as a reliable default response. Even now, when you feel like you are in control, your brain's reward centres light up, encouraging you to do more of the same. And when you feel like you are out of control, your threat mechanism is activated, motivating you to get back in control.

The unfortunate side effect of your brain's attempt to help you survive is that it will not distinguish between those things you can control and those that you cannot. It will reward your attempts to control, even if you are setting yourself up for a fall. And it will trigger your sense of threat in the face of uncertainty, trying to force you into action so you take control, even if that control is just a myth.

› the threat of the unknown

An uncertain situation leaves your neurons in limbo, unable to create a picture on which you can act. We watched this happen to a friend recently.

Monica was due to move to a new property. The house was packed in boxes, the kids had been sleeping on mattresses on the floor for two nights, and the removalist was due to arrive at 7am the next morning. At 4.30pm the afternoon before, the removalist left a message on her phone while she was out picking the kids up from school and threw all her well-organised plans into doubt: 'Sorry but our truck has broken down. We have a mechanic on the job and we're doing everything we can. It will probably be fine, but I'll call you at 6am to let you know.' Monica was thrown into panic. She tried to ring them back but there was no answer. She did circles around the house, ignoring the kids' pleas for dinner and running through all sorts of scenarios in her head. She remembers getting fixated on one silly little issue. 'All I could think of was that I had the mail diverted from tomorrow and that my mail would be arriving at an empty house. I pictured myself having to go up there and wait for the mailman to arrive so he didn't leave it in the box!'

If we could have seen inside Monica's brain during this time, we would have seen a brain struggling with uncertainty. It would have been much easier if the removalist had cancelled. Then Monica would have one thing to focus on: finding a replacement. But not knowing is much harder for the brain to handle. Electrical activity shoots down multiple pathways, trying to form a picture that makes sense. In the absence of enough information, the brain makes things up and completes the picture in many different ways. In particular, it will search for all the possible ways that the situation could unfold negatively.

There is a purpose to this focus on the negative. The brain wants you to survive and if danger is possible, it wants you to get control back fast so you are prepared for action, whether that be fight or flight. So Monica's mind was captured by the problem of her mail, whether another removalist would be available, and the flow-on effect to all the other things she had planned to coincide with her move. But the one thing that never occurred to her was that it would all be okay and that the removalist might ring at 6am with good news!

Lucky for Monica, that is what happened. And she says it was only after that call and as the day unfolded as planned, that she realised how much energy she had wasted the night before. She can laugh now about the weird ideas that went through her mind, but at the time it was the biggest problem in the world!

› brain scans show fear

Fear fills the gap left by uncertainty. Numerous studies into human behaviour, particularly our economic choices, reveal this. The Ellsberg Paradox, an experiment popularised by Daniel Ellsberg in the 1960s, explains how even the simplest of uncertainties can drive you to act on the known, in preference to the unknown. It also shows how automatic the assumption is that the unknown will be worse.

In this study, participants were seated in front of two large opaque urns. They were told that the urn on the left contained ten black marbles and ten white ones, and the urn on the right contained twenty marbles, but the proportions of black to white were not revealed. The aim of the game was to draw a black marble from one of the urns and they were free to choose from either urn. Only one chance was provided. If successful, the participant was awarded $100. Next, the challenge was to draw a white marble under the same conditions. The majority of people chose the urn on the left for both challenges. This was the urn with the known proportions of black and white marbles. The fact that most people avoided the right-hand urn altogether suggested that people have an inherent fear of the unknown and assume, consciously or otherwise, that it is a greater risk than the known.[12]

Neuro-economist Colin Camerer went further. He imaged the brains of subjects while they placed bets on whether the next card drawn from a deck of 20 cards would be red or black. The first time they played the game, the players were told how many red cards and black cards were in the deck. But the second time around it was trickier. Players were only told the total number of cards in the deck and had no idea of the proportion of red or black cards.

In the first game, players showed increased activity in the parts of the brain involved with the expectation of rewards. They were clearly calculating the odds and their expected earnings. In the second game the players' brains reacted very differently. With less information to go by, they showed substantially more activity in the amygdala, the brain's threat detector. The gap in their knowledge was filled in with fear! The *not knowing* stopped players' brains from considering the possibility of future rewards and instead, it heightened their focus on the risks associated with uncertainty.[13]

› let's make a plan

Planning is an antidote to the fear of losing control. Rather than letting your brain's energy run riot with lots of scary potential stories, planning gives it a focus that rallies its resources in a more productive way. The moment you take control of your mind and start planning, you generally feel calmer, more focused, and on track again.

Planning is good. But there is a tipping point, where planning leaves the realm of the things you can truly control and strays into those that you cannot. The moment you cross this line, you are moving away from the sort of planning that facilitates success and into the sort of planning more commonly associated with the control freak.

While uncertainty triggers the threat response, certainty generates a sense of reward. We saw this play out with an associate who took a voluntary redundancy payout. He had made this decision so he could pursue something that he was really passionate about. But when the time came to leave the old job, he jumped at the very first opportunity that came his way; a role similar to the one he had just left. Ultimately it was more comfortable for him to stick with the known, than to voyage into the unknown. He was not experiencing the freedom that comes from doing something he loved, but he was experiencing the reward of surrounding himself with certainty. His own brain had hijacked his dreams by driving him towards the safety net of feeling in control.

In our rapidly changing world, where it's impossible to predict the future, detailed planning can make you feel that you are in control. Elaborate goals, comprehensive 'to do' lists, tasks, milestones and actions are all features that focus the brain and distract it from dwelling on unknowns. But when these plans are not an appropriate response to the world around you, they can take you off the path of a well-lived life.

› your lazy brain

Once you have a plan in mind, your brain is designed to follow this path. The process of planning is like visualisation. By picturing the steps in your mind, you are wiring up the brain in the same way as if you were actually taking those steps. Your brain is learning the plan, and when the time comes to implement it, the steps come more naturally than if you had never considered the situation before. Clearly this is a great feature of our brains for more predictable situations, or ones where we can be confident that our actions will be an appropriate response to the situation.

This can be demonstrated by the famous case of Colonel George Hall. He was captured and incarcerated in a prisoner of war camp in Vietnam for seven years. Prior to the war, Colonel Hall was a golfer, playing off a handicap of four. To keep himself from going crazy in prison, every day he would visualise himself playing a round of golf at his favourite golf course. He would play each shot and each hole in his mind. When he was finally released and returned to the USA, he was invited to play in a celebrity pro-am tournament. Despite not being in the best physical condition, he hit a round of 76, which was right on his handicap. He had not held a golf club for over seven years.

It takes much less energy for the brain to follow an existing pathway than to create a new one. You may like to take the same route on a regular trip or have meals at the same time each day. In an area of the brain called the basal ganglia, all of your well-established, longstanding habits are stored. These neural circuits fire with little effort as they have been shaped with extensive training. When you activate one of these stored habits, you can feel like you are on autopilot and maybe you are. It's a great energy saving principle of the brain, but it can make your brain lazy.

During a presentation to a group of university students, one of them offered a great example of how insidious the lazy brain can be in daily life. When he and his girlfriend visit the supermarket, she often seems to be on autopilot and grabs the same products each time. One day he picked up a different bottle of sundried tomatoes suggesting they should try it instead of the usual. He was surprised by her response. She would not give it a moment's consideration and brushed him aside, moving quickly to the next aisle. He said that she is not someone that he would call a control freak in most areas of her life, but her shopping habits are a different story. He now he regularly travels the shopping aisles in front of her, holding up new products, just to get a rise out of her because he finds it so entertaining!

ᵛ ᵛ ᵛ ᵛ ᵛ

› It hit a chord with Jodie when we discussed the fear of losing control. 'I've just realised how well this describes my life. I can't remember the last time I had a weekend that was not completely planned, down to the minute. My husband is always complaining about it, but I just couldn't see what his problem was. And you know what, this is the first moment when I have realised that I don't enjoy any of it and I'm always tense because, if I'm honest, the plan never works out and I end the weekend frustrated and disappointed.'

∧ ∧ ∧ ∧ ∧

› the fight for control

Deviating from habits or plans can trigger the very uncomfortable feeling of being out of control, particularly when it feels like the change was unexpected.

∨ ∨ ∨ ∨ ∨

› As Jodie further explored her need for control, she could see that she had always been a planner, but her work had made it a much stronger habit. In her experience, it was a known fact that if you want to achieve C, you simply add A to B. She lived her life according to this formula: right job at the right time, right man at the right age, right house in the best suburb, right time to start a family. All according to a neat plan that described the ideal life ... didn't it?

Then her baby girl arrived. As every parent knows, a new baby doesn't naturally follow your plan, or even any one of the hundreds of plans in the countless baby books. For the first time in her life, Jodie felt like she had lost control. When your picture clashes with the world unfolding around you, a fight for control begins. The person with a need to control attempts to change the world to better match their internal picture. The person who can let things go will adjust their picture to align with reality. Only one of these paths offers a level of balance that can be sustained in the long run.

Jodie had never before faced a situation that did not respond to her actions. She could not comprehend any alternative, except to work harder at taking control of her baby and all aspects of this new life. She made it her mission to develop a rigid routine and to train her baby to adopt it. Eventually it worked and the baby followed the set routine. But Jodie had become an exhausted and frazzled mother who was not fulfilled by the experience of motherhood. In fact she cried nearly every second day. The gloss had come off Jodie's successful life. She felt trapped, and for the first time in her life she didn't know what she could do about it.

^ ^ ^ ^ ^

› control is the problem, not the solution

It's particularly important to distinguish here that there is nothing wrong with being in control; planning, following routines and trying to get plans back on track. In fact, these skills are essential in life. But if you don't also know when to let it go and start adapting to the situation around you, sooner or later your fear of losing control will trip you up.

One of my housemates at university showed the classic signs of being attached to control and not knowing when to let go. When we first moved in together, she was the organised one and we were all happy to let her set the rules and plans for the house. As you might expect with university students, chores were sometimes forgotten or done a little later than expected. Our organised housemate called us together and produced a nicely written roster that went up on the fridge. And we were all happy again for a couple of weeks. Then we slipped back into old habits and were swiftly called to the kitchen table for another meeting. A new roster was unveiled which was a lot more detailed: the task, the day and time it must be done, how it should be done, and how it would be checked (by our organised house mate of course). This was becoming a drag and frankly, we were starting to band together against her. It became a sport to see how long we could get away without doing our chores, before we were cornered and directed to comply with the roster. Our housemate clearly became more frustrated, the house got messier, and we became more rebellious.

I didn't understand what this all meant at the time. But I can now see that she had a picture in mind and she felt the only way to achieve this was by tightening her grip on the reins. And I can also see why we rebelled. Being controlled by another made us feel out of control, and pushing back made us feel that we were once again pulling our own reins.

Our housemate gave up first. She moved out. And we started doing the chores a bit more seriously. I now know that if we had tried a different strategy after the first roster, one where we all worked together to identify alternatives, it could have all turned out okay. In some ways, we were all captured by the need to control and it was a great big barrier.

› missing out on life

Being driven by a fear of losing control does a few things. Most importantly, it takes your attention away from what is really happening around you and this can have many undesirable consequences. By seeking to avoid uncertainty and instead creating pictures and plans in your mind, your attention is captured by those pictures and plans and does not notice new information or changing conditions. Emerging opportunities are not only missed, they might even be actively fought against, as the attachment to control causes you to focus you on how to make reality fit back into the plan.

Those who allow their fear of losing control to step in and make them hold on more tightly, rather than allow a situation to fully reveal itself, have little faith in the natural flow of life. Unwilling to let go and deal with the discomfort of uncertainty, they act too soon or too much and try to create the life pictured in their head, rather than embrace the one unfolding in front of them. Okay, you might like the picture in your head and believe that you will be happiest if that is the way life unfolds. But there are two problems with this view: the first is that you are not allowing for the possibility that other paths could make you happier, and the second is you are assuming that controlling the situation will get you there!

Life is not a machine, but that's the way a person attached to control appears to see the world. They believe this machine only operates correctly when they are in attendance pushing the right buttons, pulling the right levers, and inserting the right materials to spit out the perfect product. Because the machine of life is constantly churning, they feel they cannot rest in case a lever is missed. If things go wrong, they take hold of as many buttons and levers as they can reach and start pulling things back under control. And when things go right, they attribute it to their intervention and believe they need to do it all over again. The machine model of life might make you feel secure in the belief that you are in control, but it is an illusion. As Nelson Mandela can attest, the unknown, the unexpected, and the most feared steps in life might be the true path to freedom.

Harry likes to keep his hand on life's levers and recently explained his approach to the family football outing each weekend. 'We like to get away before the main crowd so we always leave the game when there are five minutes left on the clock. This gets us on a train without too much push and shove.' The following week was one of the most exciting games with a nailbiting finish and people still talk about it as the game of the decade. I rang Harry on the Sunday and wanted to hear all about it but he said 'We didn't see it because we had to leave to get the train.'

› training the life out of your brain

Your brain is amazing. It can process more than you might ever believe possible. And you *do not* need to be in control of it! Not only do people who are attached to control believe that they need to have their hands on life's levers at all times, they believe they must remain in control of their own brain. They try to hold on to facts, keep their lists 'top of mind', and worry if something slips into the background. Their tension is palpable because they believe that it is only by staying in control that they can produce the right answer.

Kirsty was a young leader just finding her feet in a role that required her to deliver presentations to many senior groups. She admitted that she over-prepares for these sessions. 'It's not so much on the content I am delivering that I spend too much time. It's on the possible questions they might ask. I spend so much time going over and over every angle and what I might say, it's exhausting.' She could see that logically it was not possible for her to have covered every question, no matter how long and hard she worked, but the idea of cutting back her preparation made her very anxious.

During our leadership program, she came to realise there was a big difference between ensuring she knew the important information, and training her brain to produce a series of known responses to possible questions. The first was essential but the second was constraining her ability to become effective at responding to questions on her feet. Unless she took a leap of faith and trusted her brain to deliver the information when it was needed, she would falter at the next step in her career. Kirsty needed to let go, stop tying her neurons up in knots, and allow her brain to do what it does best when it is clear, calm, and present. Maybe she could take her lead from those meditating monks!

› squeezing the life out of relationships

Our well-meaning housemate at university made us feel trapped. And we made her feel unappreciated. Relationships suffer when control oversteps its boundaries. Balance is the key. Parents must define boundaries to raise good kids. Bosses must provide structure to help people focus. Partners must give and take if they want their relationship to last. But how far do *you* go?

When control oversteps its boundaries in a relationship, you both suffer. If you're the one attached to control, you stop noticing the other person for who they really are and focus instead on trying to make them be or do what you think is right and best. Inevitably they come up short because, let's face it, every one of us is so much more complex and unique than any picture could describe. If you fear losing control, you may try harder to change them, or you may go looking for someone else you believe you can better control. The threat of the unknown and the attachment to control, convinces you that your picture is right and those who don't fit it are wrong. For you, relationships become frustrating, as your picture of what the other must be blinds you to who they really are.

If you're the one subjected to control, you might attempt to fit into their picture, or you might attempt to fight it. But all roads lead to disempowerment, disenchantment, and disappointment. Research on the effect that demanding and critical bosses have on their staff suggests that being subjected to another person's unreasonable control will ultimately weaken your mental function.[14] It's hard to claim the status of successful boss, successful parent, successful partner or successful friend when those around you feel constrained, apathetic or simply irrelevant.

The things that make life worth living don't come from completing your 'to do' list, but can often be sourced back to your relationships. Someone who values you may put you in touch with an opportunity, or an unexpected conversation can reveal vital information you had been looking for elsewhere. But it is very hard to connect and have a good relationship with a control freak. They leave little space for you to offer something up and you often feel like a pawn in their chess game.

As you let go your vision clears. No longer looking inside your head for all the answers, you become accessible to others and they become real to you. We've all seen the person glued to their mobile phone in the face of their loved ones. The father pushing their child on the swing but failing to engage with her, because he is worried that he won't be across everything at work and is frantically checking his emails. Or the parents at the school concert who are so busy trying to capture every moment through a camera so they can share them on Facebook, that they fail to connect with their child and enjoy the moment.

Any ideas you hold on how things *should be,* interfere with your ability to connect with others and what is going on around you. These thoughts become the third person in the relationship, attracting all your attention when it should be on the person in front of you.

› the final straw

There is nothing more stressful and tiring than spending day after day battling with the world and trying to reshape it to your vision. But calming your fear of losing control by rewarding your brain with a false sense of certainty will not make you happy. Looking back and realising you missed some amazing opportunities or lost some wonderful relationships probably *will* make you unhappy. But in your battle to let go, your brain, true to the Ellsberg Paradox, throws up that extra layer of protection, by convincing you that the dissatisfaction, stress, pain and unhappiness you experience now is better than the risk of the unknown pain you might experience if you release control. Remember, this is simply a trap of the brain. Even with that knowledge, so many of us will not let go until no alternative remains. Until it's the final straw.

> letting go of control (or the day i fell out of the sky)

I always believed that letting go of control was risky and, frankly, I never understood how to really do it. That was until the day I fell out of the sky. Literally. It was about 12 years ago at a time when my well-controlled world was starting to unravel. I was prepared to go with the unravelling and make some big changes, but I was still controlling things. It was time to face my fears, and when I saw people parasailing off a local beach, I realised that this was the perfect way to push myself. It was something I would normally *never* do, because a control freak will tend to avoid being tied to a boat by a rope and be left hovering above open seas!

On the way out to the launch area I drove the guys crazy, asking them all the 'what if' scenarios; a classic attempt to remove my fear of losing control by filling my head with information. 'What if the parachute breaks? Has anyone ever been injured? Are there sharks out here? Has anyone ever fallen into the ocean and had to be rescued?' The men assured me that in 20 years no-one had ever fallen out of the sky. So I was strapped in, given the thumbs up, and reeled out to the full extension of the rope.

And that's when it broke. Yes, the first time in 20 years, and it happened to me. A moment's silence, and then down I floated under the chute, straight into the ocean. My worse nightmare had just come true, but after an initial moment of disbelief, my mind said 'There is not a thing I can do about this, just let it go'. And I did. I felt a real sense of surrender and freedom. Freedom? I would not have predicted that. But in a funny way I enjoyed it and as the guys pulled me out of the water, they found me laughing and saying 'Can we do it again?!' Letting go was so much more powerful in that situation than any attempt to control would have been, and I highly recommend it.

After that event, I recognised that letting go was an effective strategy to have in my armoury. It offered an alternative in those many situations where I just did not seem to be making headway. Over time, I have found that the moment I let go in a situation where I am too attached to control, the world starts to unfold exactly as it should. I came to understand that letting go was the act of a strong person. When you release control, you can see other ways to move forward and continue towards your dreams. You realise that *how* you get there is not fixed, and that your mind's picture is only one option. In being open to taking a different path and letting go of the belief 'I am right', you find true freedom.

› in tune, not in control

People who are wired for life have an ability to adapt when things do not go to plan. Yes, they have an idea of the outcome they are looking for, but they don't think for a minute that the path to that outcome will be as they predicted. In fact, they expect the unexpected. Being unattached to their plan might just be their secret weapon for getting ahead.

The late Steve Jobs from Apple, who has been labelled one of the greatest business leaders of his time, attributed much of his success to trusting his intuition. In a 2005 Stanford University Commencement speech he explained:

'You can't connect the dots looking forward. You can only connect them looking backwards, so you have to trust that the dots will somehow connect in your future. You have to trust in something—your gut, destiny, life, karma, whatever—because believing that the dots will connect down the road will give you the confidence to follow your heart, even when it leads you off the well-worn path, and that will make all the difference.'

People who live a full life do not believe life is a machine. They allow it much more mystery and magic than that. They recognise that, like a garden, life has too much complexity and interdependence to ever be within their control, but they know that it offers all sorts of signs that only those who are alert and open-minded will notice.

Try as you might, you cannot make a tree sprout at the exact time you want it to, but you can till the soil and water the ground to help it along. Ultimately your actions are just one part of the play of life, and if you're willing to be in tune rather than in control, you'll act in ways that are more likely to make a difference. Then you can look back with satisfaction, not regret, when the final curtain drops. Surely that is one measure of a life well lived.

› the fear of standing out: it's time to find your voice

› blend in or stand out?

It was a cool evening and 22 people were sitting in a circle prior to commencing their meditation class. The teacher asked a simple question. 'What would you prefer: to blend in or to stand out?' It was unanimous: 22 out of 22 would prefer to blend in.

Now you're probably thinking to yourself: 'It depends.' Because that is the response we get from most people when we have a more in-depth chat about this question. Some say they like to stand out a bit with their clothing choices, maybe throwing on some bright colours or wild earrings, but they wouldn't sit in the front row at a comedy club. Others are quite comfortable on stage presenting to a large audience, but would decline if they were asked to be the model on the cover of their organisation's brochure. In short, each of us has our own perception of when it would be safe to stand out and when it would not.

˅ ˅ ˅ ˅ ˅

› I had always thought Sarah was confident about standing out. She looked different to the rest of us and her lifestyle was relaxed and groovy. An artist, she dedicated every spare moment of time to her passion. She desperately wanted to make it her full-time career, and used her day job purely as a means of earning an income in the interim. At the school reunion, she was very interested in how I had managed to make a success of my own business and she was keen for some advice. And she clearly had the makings of a great little business with huge potential.

I asked her how she currently sold her paintings and she explained that it was mostly through word of mouth. I asked her if she ever considered seeking media coverage and she shut that down as quickly as possible, saying that she'd rather put the money into other things. I explained that it could be quite easy to get free media and that she might easily boost her sales. Surely this would bring her dream closer to reality, then maybe she would be doing her passion full-time by the end of the year. 'All you need to do' I explained, 'is pitch yourself as a local success story.' Well, the look on her face said it all. I may as well have been asking her to jump off a cliff. She was clearly horrified at the thought. She explained that although it was her dream to be a full-time artist and generate a good living from it, she hated the thought of holding herself up as someone successful. She felt it was boastful and self-indulgent, and she didn't think she was good enough to put herself forward that way. She went on to say that she had been approached to do media interviews and also to be a guest speaker at some functions, but she always made an excuse to avoid it. She really didn't like anything that had to do with putting herself and her skills forward. 'To be honest, I feel uncomfortable charging for my work and have been told many times that my prices are too low. But I just can't make the mental adjustment.'

^ ^ ^ ^ ^

Sarah's situation is all too common. A simple opportunity to stand out can trigger a flood of anxiety and all sorts of avoidance behaviours. If you respond this way often enough, you will succeed in pushing these opportunities away and be left in peace to blend in. But is that what you really need to create the life you want?

› public and private standing out

It's easy to think this one does not apply to you, if you don't see any need to stand out in public. But there are many other situations where the fear of standing out can hinder you. Consider a lovely dinner party hosted by good friends. They invite some other friends who you've heard lots about but have not yet met. The dinner is progressing well, with lots of banter and camaraderie. It's amazing how well you're all getting along, but probably not surprising, considering you are connected through common friends. Suddenly they're all talking about a well-known public figure who you happen to have met personally and found to be really inspiring. But as you move to jump into the conversation and add your story to the mix, you realise the rest of the table is in total agreement in their opinion that this person is a real loser. In particular, the people you have just met tonight are adamant that the work this person does is basically a joke and that they should go back where they came from!! You hesitate, sit back in your chair, and say nothing. After about 20 seconds, the conversation shifts back to food and favourite restaurants. No-one seems to notice you've gone quiet and soon you are all up clearing the table and saying good night. But you can't get that moment out of your mind. The moment when you were suddenly faced with the one topic during the night on which you really held a different view. And you said nothing.

Why do we do things like this and then stay awake half the night rehearsing what we 'should have said'? We regret holding back and not being completely forthright about something we felt to be important.

We can lose our voice in many situations. Bosses might hesitate to give negative performance feedback, friends happily gossip about your failings but won't tell you to your face, and many mothers become the chronic pleaser in the family rather than have their own needs met. We want to be liked, we don't want to offend and we especially don't want to be rejected.

› safety in numbers

Belonging to a tribe was a survival strategy for our ancestors. There was safety in numbers in a world where catching big game required a team effort, the long years of child rearing benefited from an extended family, and trading resources increased your access to the essentials in life. Alone in the wilderness, with only one set of eyes searching for food and water, and no-one to keep watch while you slept, you were more likely to become a meal for a predator. There is no doubt that humans could be a threat to each other, but living in community proved the lesser of two evils.

Some of the most significant advances in human brain development occurred during this early period of society-building. Whether the brain development was the cause or the result of living in community, one thing we do know is that the human brain is a highly tuned social tool. Your brain's social skills evolved many thousands of years ago, and have been reinforced and strengthened as humans have expanded from tribes, to towns, to cities and to nations.

› belonging is a basic need

It's not surprising that the need to belong is one of your most basic needs. It is directly linked to survival. Your brain uses the same mechanisms to move you away from threats in this area as it does from others like failure and losing control. It uses fear: the fear of being left out of a group, the fear of being alone, and the fear of rejection. At its most basic level, the things that make us falter in the face of an opportunity to stand out are these fears. Rejection from the tribe would spell certain death. When your mind is running through all the excuses in the world for avoiding a situation where you could stand out, it is your brain giving you every reason to stay in the pack where it is safe.

It's not that people who are unafraid of standing out don't care about belonging or don't have the same needs as the rest of us. But through good fortune or hard work, they have rewired their mindsets. They have weakened or removed the link between standing out and being rejected, or even created a different link between standing out and positive outcomes. Maybe in the mind of Tony Robbins, opportunities to address huge audiences are linked with his passion for motivating people to really change their lives. Maybe in the mind of Lady Gaga, opportunities to shock are linked to encouraging people who feel like they don't fit in that this is okay. Many successful people have come to the conscious realisation that standing out is actually the path to achieving the important things in their lives. And many satisfied people have realised that taking a stand and being authentic clears the mind and helps them sleep at night. But many of us still feel that standing out will trigger the exact opposite: failure, humiliation and rejection.

It's worth understanding this link between your social brain, the need to belong, and the fear of standing out. Eisenberger, Lieberman and Williams conducted the first functional magnetic resonance imaging (fMRI) study of social exclusion in 2003. Three subjects in different locations were asked to play a game together over the internet, while having their brains scanned. Participants were, in fact, not playing with each other, but were playing virtual catch with two other 'participants' in a preset computer program called *Cyber Ball*. The computer was programmed so that the ball was initially thrown equally among the participants. It then changed the pattern to only throw the ball between the two fake participants, excluding the real subject from that point on. All real participants reported that they felt bothered by the exclusion, but even more striking was the increased activity in the area in their brains associated with physical pain.[15]

The way the participants' brains registered this social rejection was exactly the same way it registered physical pain. It seems that rejection really is a 'slap in the face'!

In situations of physical pain or potential physical pain, we understand that our brain is designed to trigger the threat response, precipitating fight or flight. But now we see that the brain makes no distinction between physical and social pain, so the threat response is triggered to protect you in social situations too. It's not surprising that, when facing a choice to stand out, you might stay quiet, stay in your seat, or stay in the crowd rather than risking your social acceptance and setting yourself up for rejection.

Peter was a senior manager in a large public sector organisation. During his leadership coaching with us, he revealed that situations requiring him to make presentations to an audience at work made him cold with fear. The strange thing about this was that Peter was a member of a band that played for audiences every weekend and he never felt the same fear in the band.

As we discussed this over the coming weeks, Peter described a couple of situations he had witnessed in his organisation where people who were presenting ideas they wanted to try in their area were 'hung out to dry'. It's not that any overt comments were made at the time of the presentation; in fact there was very little immediate feedback. But afterwards there were discussions behind closed doors between a few powerful people who eventually influenced the final decision. Proposals were rejected for no clear reason on a regular basis. This unseen and unspoken risk of rejection was something that Peter found particularly daunting, because he wasn't part of the power faction in the organisation and he also didn't feel that he understood what made them tick. The thought of having to make any form of presentation now filled Peter with dread. He avoided situations requiring a presentation, and had been able to convince his boss that it was best not to put him in that position. But Peter also knew this was limiting his career, and it was becoming like the metaphorical 'elephant in the room'. Sooner or later he needed to find his voice.

Peter's brain was encouraging him to stay hidden in the crowd where it was safe. He didn't want to be one of those managers who he had seen go through the pain of being left out in the cold. When he played in the band it was different. He was part of a group and his need to belong was fulfilled there. But at work he associated belonging with keeping his head down and avoiding the wrath of the power faction.

› mirroring your way to belonging

So what does it really mean to 'belong'? It means you are 'one of us', you are accepted, and at some level, it means 'you are like us'. And this is why blending in and conforming with others are behaviours we assume of someone who belongs. Once more, the social brain is at work creating this expectation, as an accidental discovery shows.

Neuroscientists in Italy were undertaking experiments in which they were monitoring a particular cell of a monkey's brain that fired only when the monkey raised its arm[16]. One version of this story has a laboratory assistant taking a break and heading out for a gelato cone (as you do in Italy!). When he returned, the monkey was still wearing the monitoring equipment and something surprising happened. When the lab assistant lifted the cone to his own mouth, activity registered on the equipment monitoring the monkey's brain. Watching someone else lift their arm triggered exactly the same reaction in the monkey's brain cell as when the monkey raised its own arm.

This was one of the first pieces of evidence that each of our brains has neurons that mimic or mirror what another person does. They are called mirror neurons and they are activated by another's actions, emotions and even their intentions. Your mirror neurons respond as if you are experiencing those thoughts, emotions or intentions yourself, creating an instant sense of shared experience. Studies on mirror neurons continue apace and their existence explains many things: why moods seem to be contagious, how we learn by watching someone else do something, why our muscles twitch when we watch a sport we love, and why I can't resist checking my phone as soon as I see someone else clicking away on theirs!

The strongest signal of blending in and belonging is surely to mirror another person's behaviour. It's so strong that our brains have hardwired it over many thousands of years. Mirroring each other was such a successful survival strategy that it takes a lot of conscious effort to resist it. Just try to avoid yawning in the face of a yawning friend!! It even happens over the phone.

You may not be aware how ubiquitous your tendency to mirror others is throughout your day. Studies suggest that we even adjust the rate at which we eat to match that of our dinner companions. It is well recognised that if you are trying to lose weight, then eat your meals with someone who makes healthy choices. If you are trying to stop smoking, don't hang out with smokers. If you want your kids to stay calm in a difficult situation, focus on being calm yourself. If you want to smile more, surround yourself with happy people.

› a group for everyone

We live in a world where there is no end to the possible groups you can join. Follow friends you have never actually met on Facebook; put a sticker on your car identifying your political allegiances; wear your team's colours to the game and you've got a new family for a few hours.

Children seek to belong early in life. They come home from their first week at school with a new best friend and then one week later it's someone else. By the time they move through high school, they usually have a core group that may last a lifetime. They experiment with sport, musical instruments, dance, language and usually stick to the one where they most like the feeling they get from being in the group. In teen years they show their group allegiance through the clothes they wear, the language they share, and the risks they are willing to take together. In childhood, the stability of belonging to the family unit is key to keeping the risk of rejection under control. A four-year-old is happy to dance around alone in front of a bunch of adults if they feel safe and loved. A 14-year-old can hardly even make eye contact with them! The teen brain looks to the peer group for its sense of belonging. The need for acceptance and approval is vital during the teen years. This is why they mimic each other relentlessly and why they feel the pain of social rejection mercilessly.

But even at this age, those who are willing to stand out and risk rejection from their group are able to do so because there is something more stirring in their mind than the brain's simple threat response. They have a sense of possibility that there is a positive outcome to be achieved from standing out and it propels them forward. In the 1997 movie *Good Will Hunting*, Matt Damon's character struggles with the implications of his natural intellect. At the age of 20, he is strongly committed to his mates, and belonging means a labouring job and a lifetime in the same neighbourhood. The life that awaits him, if he is willing to apply his mind, offers the hope of something more, a success never really dreamt of in this neighbourhood. But in standing out this way he fears that he will no longer really belong to the group, and he will risk being alone and possibly rejected. His struggle reveals the battle between the tantalising opportunity to stand out and the risk inherent in sticking your head out of the crowd.

› tall poppies

Living in Australia, we see our fair share of 'knockers'. These are the people who seem to get a sense of satisfaction from putting others down. In fact our country is famous for being afflicted with the 'tall poppy syndrome': a social phenomenon in which people of merit or talent are resented, attacked or criticised, because they stand out or appear to be elevated above their peers.

And it's not just people of talent; it's anyone who is doing something a bit different. This was evident in a team-building program we ran for a national company. During the event the participants were paired up and each pair cooked a meal for the group at some point during the program. The activity wasn't just about the food, it was really about being creative and offering a unique experience to the whole team. One of the pairs really shone. They had costumes, music, and served their food in very unique ways. As they presented it to the group, we watched the dynamics. There were sniggers, eye rolls, and derogatory quips from a small gang who looked to others in the group as if to say 'Are you one of us or one of them?' As well as cutting the pair down, they were trying to herd the wider group together. Most laughed along with them to some extent, but during the next break we could hear most of the group talking about how rude that gang had been and that their behaviour was inappropriate. But no-one stood up and addressed the issue head on. The fear of standing out and the need to belong, even to a dysfunctional team, was too strong.

› when belonging is not good for you

Belonging to a group is good. Feeling the sense of camaraderie that comes from connecting with people who think, feel and act like you is an essential human need. It helps you to survive, and it enables you to thrive. Beyond the argument for safety in numbers, is a recognition that great relationships are the key to your emotional health. But a relationship is not great unless it allows you to be and become your very best, even if that means going against the tide. The best relationships give you the confidence to step into the unknown and trust that those you have left behind support you and feel proud of you. Belonging is only good for you when it allows you to find your voice, not when it seeks to silence your truth.

› divide and conquer

The fear of rejection can drive you to conform to people or groups who do not have your best interests at heart. When kids band together to bully a schoolmate, most of them are just mirroring the behaviour of a few. They feel it's safer to join the bully, copy their behaviour and belong to this group than to stand out and risk the group turning on them. Whenever you seek your sense of belonging by joining with those who put others down, your fear is taking you down the wrong path.

In 2011, Brisbane hosted the popular two-day conference *Happiness & Its Causes*. It attracted thousands of participants and was held at the largest Convention Centre in town. Not only were many of the speakers internationally recognised scientists and experts on emotion and human behaviour, but His Holiness the Dalai Lama was also a key draw card. Clearly this was a popular event, and it was attended by people from many mainstream walks of life, including a large proportion of business people.

On the morning of the second day, there was an unrelated breakfast held in the room above the conference, at which a local politician was speaking. The event was attended by corporate types, some of whom were also attending *Happiness & It Causes*. While no-one would be surprised that a politician was at ease in front of an audience, he still sought to identify with the group in front of him. His opening joke denigrated the event going on downstairs. Clearly he assumed that the type of people he had in his audience would think the conference trite and irrelevant in their world. But he underestimated this group. In his attempt to bond with them, he actually triggered the opposite reaction in many of the listeners. In fact, his joke was enough for many to say that it had completely changed their view of this politician and their respect had been lost.

› holding back

You cannot be successful in your attempts to stand out, if you are only prepared to go half way. If there remains some truth that you are more focused on the need to belong than you are on stepping up to the plate, you will be found out. The social brain's radar is highly attuned. It can sense good intentions, authenticity and humility, and it can also sense falseness, manipulation and doubt. This capability may explain why we retain a healthy scepticism around the promises of politicians, advertisements and salespeople!

When you deceive yourself and believe you can grab an opportunity to stand out, but then do not do it the justice it deserves, you will achieve little. Unfortunately this can simply reinforce the fear for next time, increasing the likelihood you might give up and fall back into the crowd.

˅ ˅ ˅ ˅ ˅

› Sarah was asked to talk to a class of art students about what it is like to be an artist. I suggested that she tell the group some stories from her life, something with which she could feel comfortable and familiar. She asked me to watch her practise her delivery. I sat mesmerised for the next three minutes as she wove a tale that was clear, simple and powerful. 'You've nailed it! There's nothing I would suggest you change. Just do it like that and they will get so much out of it.' Later that day, I went to watch her. As two other artists took the stage and delivered their story, the group laughed and clapped in admiration. Sarah rose from her seat and was the last to speak. I noticed she looked nervous and she was fiddling with her papers. And I listened with a little sadness, as she told a story that was stilted and missing many of the original ingredients. The group clapped politely and she gave a brief smile and sat down. I managed to sidle up to her later and gently asked why she had changed direction. She said 'I don't know. I just got really nervous because no-one else had done anything like mine, so I thought they would just laugh at me.' Sensing the threat of rejection, her brain had triggered a flight response, which manifested in her holding back. Sarah knew she had missed an opportunity, and she admitted the next time we met that she had experienced a sleepless night full of 'if only' thoughts.

˄ ˄ ˄ ˄ ˄

› trying too hard

Yes, you need to make a connection with others; and the best way to do that is to focus them on something you have in common. But if you are more concerned about being accepted than you are about being true to your message, others will sense this imbalance. In an effort to win approval, it is possible to try too hard and to push people away rather than bring them in closer. I saw this recently in a charity organisation that brought women together to help disadvantaged women in another country. They formed a Board and every person wanted to be there to make a difference. But the Board achieved little, and slowly people resigned until no-one was left. The problem was that the organisers were so grateful to the people volunteering for the Board, they put all their energy into winning their approval rather than letting them truly contribute. Meetings would be spent trying to make Board members feel important, rather than getting on with the job. This ultimately drove everyone away.

› now is the time to stand out

Casey Heynes was the boy who fought back. In 2010, after years of bullying from fellow students, Casey hit back. The difference between this, and situations occurring all over the world each day, is that someone videoed this event and posted it on You Tube. Much was made of the moment when a young boy decided that he would stand up for himself. But the thing that made Casey truly stand out, was that he found a way to use his new profile for good. He motivated action on bullying and gave many other kids hope. His authenticity and good intentions meant that, rather than rejection, he was embraced and supported.

Standing out offers you the chance to be heard. Whether it's a conversation around the dinner table where you do not shy away from stating your beliefs, or an international stage where you put a case for change, embracing opportunities to stand out is worth the risk. It doesn't always lead to applause and acclaim. In fact, it well might fall flat and people will roll their eyes. But you won't get eaten by wolves and there will still be people who think 'Good on you.'

Your willingness to find your voice and be authentic can open new doors, deliver life lessons, and bring the sort of peace of mind and satisfaction that comes from living a full life.

› establishing your presence

Standing out has become harder to achieve in this hectic, busy world. Imagine you have just started a home business. You decide that you need to advertise to get some customers. You have purchased a database of 5,000 people and you are going to email out an advertisement.

How effective do you think this will be? Based on experience, you would be lucky to have one person respond. This sounds tough, but consider for a moment the world we live in. To say we experience information overload would be an understatement. People report receiving an average of 40 emails a day, and most of the people we know exclaim that 40 would be luxury! On top of that, you receive information from multiple sources: television, radio, internet, your friends and family. Can you imagine what you need to do to get noticed?

We have so many options these days. Walk down the breakfast cereal aisle and see how many products there are compared to 20 years ago. Research has found that brain function will diminish when faced with too many choices, making it difficult to focus effectively on daily tasks. And too much choice often results in consumers making no choice at all.[17] Information is everywhere and the choices are abundant.

So, if you want to stand out in this busy, crowded world, you need to be authentic and find your own voice. Bloggers who start posting information because they are passionate about a topic, seem to gather a more enthusiastic following than those who do it with a plan to make money. Budding vocal artists launch their own careers on You Tube and have millions of fans before a record company even looks at them. Following the herd offers safety in numbers, but it rarely leads to life well lived. In fact, it often results in mediocrity.

You need to stand out from the crowd. That doesn't mean just doing what others are doing, but doing it better. It means doing it differently with your own authentic style. Jack is in the travel industry. He saw an ad for his dream job representing Australia in international tourism. The job asked for a resumé and a standard application form. Knowing that the job would attract hundreds or maybe thousands of applicants, he decided to apply for it in a different way. He made a video addressing all of the questions on the application form and included testimonials from clients. Then he wrapped his resumé around some bottles of an iconic Australian beverage, and delivered the whole package to the recruiter. The recruiter got so many resumés that it wasn't even possible to look at many of them for longer than a minute. But there was one that she paid attention to. And now Jack is sitting in his dream job.

› rejection happens

I was recently at a conference, where there were some unexpected performers in the exhibition area during breaks. The space was relatively empty, when we saw a woman holding a microphone at the end of the room. As her colleague joined her, they started singing and rapping. It was incongruous in this situation. Initially I could feel my body respond with that cringing feeling that tells you your mirror neurons are firing a warning message that this is a high-risk situation. I moved myself against a wall so as not to stand out. But why? No-one was looking at me.

Even when we are alert to the cause of this fear of standing out, we can't help but feel its effects. And the truth is that being rejected is a reality and it will happen. But you do not need to fear it. The fear is the thing that holds you back. Potential rejection is all around. One person hates your idea and the next person loves it. One rejection does not banish you for all time to the wilderness. Those who can feel the fear, and do it anyway, are the ones who find their authentic voice and grow.

Lady Gaga is an example of someone who, through standing out, has achieved more than success. Her flamboyant wardrobe and stage antics certainly make her stand out from the crowd everywhere she goes. Many of us would find her very strange and feel the strong urge to reject her. But whatever you think of her, the truth is that she is incredibly successful, not just because of her talent, but because she found her own authentic way to stand out. And it resonates with many millions of people. For a long time she was a song writer for other successful artists, but then she transformed herself to one of the bestselling artists of all time. Her infamous *Monster Ball Tour* was not only the highest grossing concert tour of all time, but it created tribes of disciples affectionately called 'Little Monsters'. Lady Gaga is not just a music artist to them. She is someone who gives them permission to be different and, by doing this, she fulfils their need to belong.

› success through purpose

Fear takes over when you give it too much attention. When you set your own mindsets aside and focus instead on a purpose, the needs around you, and the way things are unfolding, you are more likely to act in ways that make a real difference. People who struggle to be fulfilled with their lives, whether personally or professionally, are often consumed by thoughts about themselves and what it all means to them. They are blind to opportunities, or fail to grab them with open arms. People who are wired for life remind themselves why they are doing something, and how it makes a difference to the people around them.

For some people, this sense of purpose is thrust upon them, forcing them to find their voice through personal tragedy. Walter Mikac started the *Alannah and Madeline Foundation* after his two girls were tragically killed in the Port Arthur shootings in 1996. Famous Australian cricketer Glenn McGrath continues at the helm of one of the most successful breast cancer foundations in memory of his late wife, Jane. People often emerge from a tragic ordeal with a need to help others. They overcome the fear of standing out, because their sights are set on something much more important than their own survival. Contributing to a strong purpose leads to one of the rare times that a sense of reward will overtake the fear of a threat. But you can do this without suffering a catastrophic event. All you need to do is focus on contributing to something that makes a real difference.

I can vividly recall a particular time when I was paralysed with the fear of standing out. I was sitting in my car on the side of the road after receiving a call from my PR agent. We were running a campaign, and a television station wanted to interview me in a broadcast that would go national that evening. I responded with mild panic and my brain was throwing up excuses why I couldn't do it. The PR agent was confused by my reaction and said 'You *do* realise you are running a campaign that was designed to put you on television in front of millions of viewers worldwide don't you?'.

At that point I realised how ridiculous my reaction was. I really wanted to achieve this goal of getting international exposure for a message I believed could change lives. I knew this was a great opportunity, but my mind felt the need to protect me. You see, all of a sudden it became about me, not the messages I was trying to spread. Me being watched by a million people. Me and how I'd be perceived. Me and whether I would slip up. My purpose went straight out the window. Once I reminded myself about the purpose of the campaign, my fear dissipated and I was able to grab the opportunity with open arms. We have a purpose of cultivating consciousness and this cannot be done if you are too afraid to talk to people. When I focus on 'cultivating consciousness' any fear takes a back seat.

When you succumb to the fear of standing out, you will always limit what is possible. Just as the person who will only travel on a dual carriageway misses the magic to be found on the less travelled roads, avoiding opportunities to stand out cuts off many paths. In the quiet safety of blending in and conforming with others, you risk a much greater peril: the risk of losing yourself. To live an authentic life you need to find your voice. We all have a purpose, message or strengths to contribute to the world. By letting these shine, you will experience a life filled with contentment and meaning.

› the fear of missing out: it's time to think abundantly

› it should have been me!

Have you had that twisting feeling in the pit of your stomach, when you hear news that someone has been recognised for something that you have been aspiring to yourself? Maybe a manager has praised another team member for a good idea and you've said to yourself 'I was thinking about something like that' while you stare daggers at the praised staff member. Or someone launches a product in your industry that your clients are raving about, and you feel the niggling fear that you have missed the boat. Or maybe you have just heard that your friend is getting married or having a baby, and the fact that it hasn't happened for you taints your happiness for her.

We have an incredibly supportive friend (actually we have many and we're very grateful for them all!) but this particular friend is like a mother lion protecting her cubs. While she is our loudest and most enthusiastic champion, the flipside of this passion is that she is quick to attack any person or company who do similar work to us. She'll scoff at reviews of new books, be scathing about the performance of an expert on morning TV, and deride the list of speakers for conferences. She always says 'It should be you!' and clearly feels that the success of others reduces the chances of us achieving the same. While her response is born out of a desire to lift us up, her behaviours show that she really only believes that can happen if others are pulled down. Her mindset is one of scarcity and the fear of missing out. It's a belief that there is only a limited amount (of market share, attention, money, happiness, love) to go around, and every time someone else gets some of it, there is less for us.

The fear of missing out manifests itself in many different forms. I met someone recently in a mothers' group, who desperately tries to win the approval of others. She constantly organises coffee dates with other mothers and tries desperately hard to forge a close relationship with everyone she meets. She claims to be loved by everyone she knows. Initially I thought she simply had a strong need to belong, but then I saw another side to her. She relishes pointing out to others that she has been invited or included in something, when they have been left out. She highlights the faults in other people's children, while waxing lyrical about her own. She finds ways to assert that the teachers of her own children's classes are better than the other teachers.

People started avoiding her and, rather than winning the love and acceptance of others, she was considered selfish and rude. But in truth, she suffered from the fear of missing out. It turned out that she'd had a difficult upbringing and had to fight to get her share of everything, including the attention and approval of her parents. Raised to believe everything was scarce, and that survival depended on beating others to resources, she saw things only as win/lose.

The fear of missing out stems from a belief that there is not enough to go around. A child's birthday cake cut into eight pieces, when there are nine children, can ruin the day. No-one really wants to share their piece; in fact, they think it's unfair that they should be expected to do so. So where does this fear of missing out really come from and why do we react so strongly when we think there's not enough to go around?

› brain on scarcity alert

Do you think you could survive if you were dropped in the desert, the jungle or on a deserted island, with no hope of rescue and no modern tools at your disposal? Many people doubt they would last too long, and it's hard to imagine what you would do to make it through. Even Tom Hanks in the movie *Castaway* could pilfer some useful material from the cargo of his broken aircraft!

But the earliest humans faced this situation every day and survived only on their wits. The greatest threat to survival was surely lack of access to food, water and materials for shelter. The changing seasons and the changing fortunes of a landscape could have had a significant impact on how plentiful or scarce these resources were. Scarcity, and the threat of future scarcity, loomed constantly and the human brain evolved to respond to this threat in its usual way: flight or fight. Nomadic tribes moved from place to place at the whim of local conditions. But others chose to insure against these risks and guarantee their access to vital resources in other ways. The threat of scarcity and the fear of missing out taught humans the skills of hoarding, theft and warfare, trickery, manipulation and lying. The threat of scarcity was probably the incubator for cultivating 'either/or' thinking, a 'win/lose' mentality, and the dominance of competition over cooperation in the human brain.

Today the threat of scarcity and the fear of missing out goes well beyond getting enough food, water and the basic essentials of life. Your brain triggers the fear of missing out at any sign of scarce resources, but also at any signal that something may become unavailable, whether you really need it or not.

› i want that one!

Have you ever bought something just because it was your last chance to get it, even though you didn't really need or want it? In the 1960s, a city in Florida banned phosphates for environmental reasons. This meant that some popular brands of detergent would be pulled off the shelf. Phosphates had no impact on the cleaning capability of detergent and those with the phosphates were no more effective than those without. But in the weeks before the ban went into effect, stores experienced massive sales in the detergents with phosphates, and in the weeks *after* the ban took effect, people were travelling beyond the city limits and buying up the detergents wherever they could be found. People wanted the banned detergents, not because they were more effective cleaning agents, but because they had become scarce.

It's the classic case of 'reverse psychology'. Denying something makes people want it more. It's called reactance, and it kicks in when people feel that the 'missing out' is unfair. Constraining someone's choice, but more importantly their freedom to choose, triggers a reaction designed to reassert one's freedoms.

Imagine you are walking through the city and see a crowd gathering around people in red T-shirts handing something out. Your brain draws your attention to this situation and entices you towards it for two reasons: the threat alert says check it out, and your mirror neurons want to mimic the behaviour. Without much conscious thought, you redirect your path to ensure you pass closely by and can stick your hand out if it's something of interest. But you see that they are handing out 'how to vote' cards for the coming election and you're simply not interested. Your brain switches off and you're back on your way. But what if they were handing out free lottery tickets for Saturday's draw? And as you get close and put out your hand they say 'Sorry, we're only giving these to people walking with children.' 'But I have children too!' you exclaim, looking around to see how many other people think this is unfair.

Your brain is highly sensitive to unfairness. A perceived injustice or feeling 'left out' triggers the same networks as physical pain and switches on your threat alert. Suddenly you become very 'me' focused, defensive and prepared for battle. Even your friends saying 'Oh well, better luck next time' just seems like a further affront. But let's take a clear look at this situation. Did you really miss out on something? If you had walked up a different road you would never even have known the lottery tickets were being handed out. And would the luck of the people who did receive one suddenly make you an unlucky person? And just one more point: what are the odds of one of those lottery tickets actually being the winning ticket? But even in the face of all this logic, your brain can still make you feel that you have missed out and it's just not fair.

› it must be good

There are numerous experiments testing reactance and the impact that triggering the fear of missing out can have on behaviour. Even a previously undesired object can become the most popular item, if this brain response is triggered. Wilson and Lassiter[18] conducted an experiment with a group of children, first identifying a toy that none of the children played with in free play. One group was then told they were allowed to play with any toy, including this unused toy. The second group was told they could play with any toy but NOT that toy. Later both groups were given an opportunity to play with the subject toy. The second group spent twice as long playing with it as the first group, the denial making it suddenly of value. And experiments with adults show the same response in similar situations. This is a wired default pathway that would have served the survival of our ancestors, but now just makes us seem terribly irrational.

The sales industry thrives on the fact that scarcity makes things more desirable. You hear the talk all the time: 'This is the last one in that size', 'It will only be that price until tomorrow', 'Someone else has made an offer on that house, so you'd better put your best offer in.' How often have you responded to it? We had an experience with this recently when we were selling our *Mind Gardener Guides* at a conference. We had taken a smaller number of the *Great Relationships Guide* and they sold out quickly. We put up a 'sold out' sign and made it clear we were taking orders. Well, all of a sudden they became hot property. Even people who were buying another guide, and hadn't looked at the *Great Relationships Guide*, suddenly wanted it.

It's a bit like the girl or guy who plays hard to get. Suddenly everyone is glancing their way. Want to get your partner to commit? Break up with them. They will agree to anything just to get you back. But that's the problem with the scarcity strategy. People respond out of a desire to avoid the threat of missing out, not out of a genuine desire to make this choice. The scarcity strategy is a dangerous path if you really want fulfilment.

› you can't have it all, or can you?

Apart from making you buy things you don't need and make choices you didn't really want, the fear of missing out can drive you to make trade-offs that are unnecessary. Comments like 'I'm putting it all into my work now. I can relax later' or 'I'll travel and do the things I love when I retire' reveal a wiring that assumes you can't have it all. Too many people delay one desire for another and regret it later. We know a few women who delayed having a baby until they were financially secure, then found they could not get pregnant.

We fear missing out so much that we are prepared to negotiate with the world to limit our losses. Believing that you can't have it all forces a choice: *I'll take status first, then I'll have money, then freedom, then happiness.* But have you ever stopped to ask yourself if this is necessary? Does the evidence really suggest that it is not possible to be successful, fulfilled and happy all at the same time?

Sure you can point to examples of people who don't have it all, but maybe that's because they too are trapped by this 'either/or' thinking. The unfortunate thing is that when this is the dominant mindset in a group, a company, or even a whole country, the belief is reinforced through your mirror neurons. When the people around you live their life a certain way, they lay a path not just by example, but literally in your brain. It becomes hard to see there could be another way. But there are always examples of people who think differently and live a full life unaffected by scarcity. We'd prefer to switch our mirror neurons on to them, the ones who have discovered that the fear of missing out is a trap, and that there is better mindset: to think abundantly.

› there is enough

When you see someone else experience happiness, rather than reducing your changes of experiencing it, it actually gives you a boost. Researchers at the Harvard Medical School and the University of California[19] have proved that your emotional state can be affected by those three degrees separated from you. If you live within a mile of a happy friend, your chances of happiness are increased by 25 per cent. A co-resident spouse experiences an

8 per cent increased chance, siblings living within a mile have a 14 per cent increased chance and neighbours 34 per cent!

If you were raised in a loving home, you are more likely to create a home full of love when you have your own family. Those who love fully are not losing anything by giving their love away. They generate warm emotional responses from all who meet them and they draw love to themselves. To believe that opportunities for love run out at a certain age, or after a relationship ends, is to look at love as a finite resource rather than the abundant one that it actually is.

There is also no limit on creativity, charity, fun and peace. Ideas spawn more ideas, giving promotes giving, one person's effort encourages the effort of others, and success breeds success. In business, those who think abundantly celebrate the success of other people in their field, believing that one person's success can benefit others. So called competitors find ways to share information and opportunities, recognising that cooperation can increase the chances of success for them both.

I saw an example of this on a recent trip to Spain. After a busy day of sightseeing, my partner and I decided to have a casual dinner in our room, so we wandered through the local market to source provisions. We stopped at a bread stall that had just what we were after, but the stall was unattended. We were about to walk on when a stallholder from across the corridor rushed over and served us. As he came over I could see that he also stocked bread on his side, but instead of trying to divert us there, he wrapped the bread and took our money and placed it in the first stallholder's tin. It was clear that this market was a true community, where people helped each other to achieve success, rather than being driven by personal or competitive motives. They clearly believed that there was plenty to go around and that, by helping each other, they could all win.

Sure, some things in our world are finite. On a serious note, there continue to be places where access to the bare essentials is difficult and the fear of missing out is a valid concern. But if you're reading this book, we guess this is not you. Once you get your priorities right, 'hard sell' strategies are less likely to trap you, because you realise the important things in life are love, happiness and making a difference. These things are not depleted by use, but are in fact expanded every time someone activates them.

› scarcity lowers your iq

Imagine we set you the challenge to establish a business with $100,000. What goes through your head? What plans, ideas and opportunities would you pursue? Now imagine a different challenge. Establish the business, but you only have $1,000. How different is your thinking? With the larger sum to invest, you probably felt free to be quite creative with ideas. With the lesser figure you may have felt restricted and cautious.

Eldar Shafir of Princeton and Sendhil Mullainathan of Harvard[20] conducted a study that revealed how scarcity impacts cognitive abilities. They conducted a battery of IQ tests with Indian sugar farmers, at two different phases of their work cycle. The first was after they sold their harvest, a time when they live in relative prosperity. The second was before harvest when they live with scarcity. During the first phase they performed very well on the tests, but their performance declined during the second phase. The study found they become more short-sighted and had trouble controlling their attention. When times are tough people worry, thinking harder about every decision and every choice. Prosperity frees you from these concerns and frees your brain's resources to attend to more complex and higher order matters.

You don't have to be facing real scarcity to suffer these effects to your cognitive abilities. As we've seen from the studies where the scarcity threat is triggered falsely, simply thinking you might be missing out is enough to trip you up on your path through life. When your default pathways take over, your brain pushes you to focus on the threat, to the detriment of all else. The likely behaviour is to take too much, keep things to yourself, and become defensive, protective and guarded.

› missed opportunities

When you try to build your success and happiness on a scarcity mindset, you are driven by fear (of missing the opportunity), or by aggression (against perceived competitors) or by protectiveness (that others are taking what should be yours). When your brain is in any of these states, it fixates on the threat and your focus becomes narrowed by the effects of stress. Many of the brain functions that are crucial for making good balanced decisions are switched off. Rather than being creative and focusing on what you are really trying to achieve, decisions are made based on what others are doing, and many great opportunities are missed.

David was one of our clients who worked in a marketing company. He was always worried about his future income sources and displayed the anxiety of one who believed there was not enough to go around. When we first started working with him, he was keen to secure a contract with a large company that just happened to be another of our clients. Josh was the decision-maker on the contract and David had the opportunity to present his proposal to Josh and two other representatives. A few days after the presentation, David phoned me. Knowing I had a great relationship with Josh, he said he would really appreciate me identifying any opportunity to connect with him again. The following Monday I ran into Josh in the corridor. He greeted me saying 'Hey, I saw your mate David at a networking event on Friday night and gave him a wave. I don't think he remembered who I was because he just kept walking!' He expressed a concern that David didn't seem very client focused.

I immediately knew exactly what had happened. David would have turned up at the networking event, hell bent on meeting as many people as possible. Driven by the fear of missing out, he would have wanted to cover the whole room but, fixated on this goal, he completely missed the opportunity he so desperately wanted with Josh.

In the consulting industry, you often find that the consultants who constantly worry about their next dollar struggle to find work, and those who never worry are always busy. If your attention is distracted by the fear of missing out, your focus narrows and you miss opportunities emerging from unexpected quarters.

› competition or cooperation?

Charles Darwin's evolution principles are used to justify the importance of competition and survival of the fittest. But it is often overlooked that cooperation is the true key to survival, evolution and growth. Species cooperate all the time, both among each other and with other species. There is nothing more fascinating than to see the incongruous matching of a small and large animal, each fulfilling their roles in harmony. Small cleaner fish swim in and out of the mouths of their large client fish, ridding them of bacteria. Just one swallow would provide the client fish with a meal, but the capacity for cooperation results in a more effective long-term reward for them both: a meal for the small cleaner fish and a clean mouth for the larger client. In Africa, large animals such as giraffe and cattle cooperate with a bird called the ox-pecker. The bird travels on their back, grooming them and also warning of approaching danger.

Cooperation is a constant, while competition is situation-dependent. It arises specifically when resources are scarce, and when more animals are competing for the same resources. Animals can move from competition and back into cooperative relationships as dictated by their environment and their needs, but we humans are not so adaptable. Competitive people tend to be competitive for life, treating every situation as a battle to be won. We need pathways in our brain to respond both competitively and cooperatively, and we need the clarity to see when each is appropriate.

The reality is that the principles of living systems rule the world, and the rules apply to us without exception. The society and communities you live in are interconnected. Just as the extinction of a fish species will have a corresponding negative affect on all the other species in that region, so too a whole community is affected when one part of the community fails. Country towns decline when essential services like banks, police and post are shut down. On the flip side, when every part of the community works together, the whole community flourishes.

We heard a story about how one person's actions changed the fortunes of a whole city suburb. The suburb was suffering from an increase in juvenile crime and drugs. Unemployment and truancy were high, and kids had too much time to get up to mischief. The police had tried everything and teachers had implemented strategies to no avail. Business owners were getting increasingly frustrated at the graffiti and theft, but there seemed to be nowhere to turn. Then one business person made a move that changed everything. She funded two factories, recruited only local unemployed people, and started an apprenticeship program to get troubled youth into the workforce. For the first time, the police and local schools worked together as they helped her identify candidates. The program was a huge success. Over time, crime rates plummeted, youth self-esteem climbed and education averages rose as the young people either left school for work or made a conscious decision to study harder. The suburb came alive again, and the business woman recovered her investment. It seemed like solving a problem in one area had a flow-on effect to other areas and benefited all.

There are many examples of how a person's generous actions reap benefits for the receiver and the giver. There are equally as many cases where self-centred actions create disadvantage for many. I experienced this firsthand, when I was in a major traffic jam on my way to work recently. I was travelling on my usual route at the usual time, but something was very different. I finally realised what it was. People attempting to merge were being met by some unusually stubborn drivers who didn't want to let them in. This self-centred action caused the traffic to build up for kilometres. The mentality that 'I need to get to the city quickly, so I can't let anyone else in' was in fact making it slower for everyone. On other days the traffic flows beautifully, people merge effortlessly, and all keep to the speed limit.

Traffic is a great analogy for the flow of life. Cooperation keeps us all moving forward, but competition can bring us all to a grinding halt. Collectively, we can achieve much more than we can alone.

∨ ∨ ∨ ∨ ∨

> Since reconnecting with Bill at the school reunion, I had thought a few times about how nice it must be to live at the beach and be out of the rat race. When we met up a few weeks later, he confirmed that part of his reason for making such a big change was his desire to get away from the competitive world of politics and the pressure it created. But the stories he told about his first few months, indicated

how difficult he had found it to let go of the 'win/lose' and 'either/or' mentality. He told me this story.

One morning when he was opening his store, he noticed that the shop two doors down had been leased. A customer informed him that a local person called Tom intended opening a shop that sounded a lot like Bill's in a few weeks. Bill was wild. His first thought was 'how could Tom do this to me?' He avoided Tom for a week and spent every waking moment plotting how he could thwart Tom's plans. It was only after a number of sleepless nights, that Bill realised these emotions were all symptoms of the very mindset that he had wanted to avoid. So he asked himself 'Why am I assuming this will have a negative impact? How would I react if I assumed there was enough here for both of us?' From that moment on he changed his course of action. He met with Tom seeking to better understand Tom's motivation. And they found a way to specialise each of their businesses in a non-competitive way.

As a result they actually attracted more customers to the area. Two shops selling complementary products created a 'hub' that people travelled to for all their needs. By specialising his products, Bill actually identified some services that he could add. Doing these things also made him feel fulfilled and gave him a sense of purpose that had been missing for some time. The introduction of another store had seemed like the end of the world, but it was actually the beginning of a whole new world.

∧ ∧ ∧ ∧ ∧

Competition is a short-term view. If you win at the expense of someone else, you increase the chances of all losing in the future.

There is always another way to see things and this can open up a world of opportunity.

› win-win-win

Connections are strengthened when we help each other. When you renovate your home, you can waste countless hours searching for a good electrician, or you can ask a friend or associate and get a personal recommendation within minutes. How many times has someone in your own network unexpectedly helped you achieve one of your goals?

The scarcity mentality can cause people to turn their backs on others, driven by the belief that if they help someone else, they will be disadvantaged. As a young graduate entering a male-dominated organisation, I looked up to the senior women who had 'made it.' They were role models and symbols of possibility. I decided that I would approach one of the women I admired, to take on an informal mentoring relationship with me. I didn't want much of her time, just some informal advice every now and then. Imagine my surprise when, on making my request, she rejected me! Too busy. Too hard. A few weeks more in my job and I started to hear more about this person and other people's experiences with her. She had a reputation for being particularly harsh on other women. She set higher standards for the women in her team and was more relaxed with the men. She was once quoted as saying that she worked hard on her own to break through the glass ceiling, and others should do the same. So maybe she wasn't too busy, just too threatened.

Senior people often try to keep junior people down. But successful people say that one of the secrets of their success is to surround themselves with good people. Nurturing the enthusiasm of a young person with talent is smart. Cooperating in this way delivers results for the boss, the young person and the company. A win-win-win!

› the brain has a drive to be altruistic

A number of studies show that the brain's reward centres light up when acting altruistically.[21] But a perceived threat will pull rank, stealing your attention away from these positive and appealing activities, to deal with potential survival needs. This is why it is so important to be conscious of your brain's patterns. If you have a habitual pattern that assumes threat, even where there is none, you may never be released from this threat response long enough to engage in something that will give you a true sense of fulfilment.

When threat and the thought of threat is removed, people appear to be spontaneously altruistic. Never was this more apparent than in the 2011 floods in our hometown, Brisbane. Most watched horrified as many suburbs were inundated, while others remained completely untouched. It was surreal to sit under a blue sky watching news updates, showing people just a few kilometers away losing their homes and possessions, as the river slowly rose. The city was at a standstill and people were in shock. Within hours of the river receding, the Brisbane community came out in droves with buckets, shovels and anything else they could grab on their way out the door. Thousands of people headed to the affected suburbs and just started cleaning mud out of people's houses, helping in any way they could. They were called the *Mud Army* and their actions were reported around the world. When faced with no threat to themselves, these people's brains desired only to help others and it was an inspiration.

Last time I checked, more than one person can be successful, fulfilled, happy, secure a great opportunity, or get a lucky break. Assuming such things are scarce, creates the impression that you only have one shot at succeeding in life. But when you think abundantly, you switch off the fear response and your world opens up. There really is enough of the truly great things to go around. As Charles Darwin said: 'The vigorous, the healthy, and the happy survive and multiply.'

› the fear of facing the truth: it's time to take responsibility

› gratitude in despair

In 2011, not only did a flood affect much of Queensland's capital city, Brisbane, but within the month a cyclone knocked down the small beachside town of Tully Heads. Many people lost everything, so we were surprised when we received this email:

'Our household has two of your wonderful Mind Gardener guides, *The Clear Mind Guide* and *The Living Happy Guide*. Recently we were evacuated from our house as Cyclone Yasi approached the Queensland coastline. I made sure both guides were packed along with our photos and hard drives filled with digital files documenting our lives so far. That's how much we love them and you! Thank you for being you.'

Receiving this message was the ultimate compliment, but aside from that we were inspired by the actions of this amazing woman. Faced with crisis and potential disaster, she had the foresight to recognise the importance of maintaining the mental health of her family.

The email went further:

'We have been surrounded by the most amazing family and friends since we began preparing for this event. Last weekend we visited what was left of our beautiful neighbourhood and began the process of "red tape" ... all positive so far! Today we began the process of relocating ourselves and our boys to a new "temporary" life in the far north. At the moment we're scared from the uncertainty, there's no denying that, but with the help of people like yourself, we believe our experience will make us stronger and more positive with life, love and friendship. So really, we're the lucky ones cause isn't that what life is all about?'

This woman lost everything in the disaster and had to relocate her family 2,000kms away. She could easily be forgiven for feeling angry, hopeless and all but giving up. But no, she was grateful! When your life is in total disarray would you take the time to write 'thank you' letters to people? This inspirational woman is no victim. She is a perfect example of someone who looks life right in the face and takes responsibility for how she responds to what she finds there.

› the victim mentality

'Why do these things always happen to me?' This question is a sure sign that the victim mentality is at play. In your circle of friends and associates you probably see examples of the victim mentality more than you realise. A friend who continuously goes for 'bad boys' then wonders why she keeps getting hurt. A mate who complains he's badly done by at work, but has said the same thing about his last three jobs. Or the person who whinges about always running late, and blames the government: not enough public transport, poor roads, too much traffic.

When someone believes that external factors are responsible for their dissatisfaction and that someone else is to blame for the position in which they find themselves, they are embracing the role of the victim. Believing themselves to be powerless to change their circumstances, frustration, anger, confusion or distress is directed outward, and onto any target other than themselves.

The victim mentality is a case of a misdirected threat response in the brain. When you operate with a belief that something is being done *to* you, your brain switches on its threat response and targets the perceived threat. While throwing accusations around seems like a fight response: 'They did this to me and I want them to pay', the victim mentality is actually a flight response, a way to avoid taking responsibility for how you deal with difficult circumstances. The real threat for the victim is their own paralysis, brought on by a mindset that looks outward and not at the only thing you really control: yourself.

› you can't handle the truth

'Mother in court claims: Major fast food chain responsible for my child's obesity.' This is a fairly typical newspaper headline in this day and age. In fact, we see people playing the role of the victim throughout society daily. In our increasingly litigious world, there are some outrageous claims and growing evidence that people are losing the skill of taking responsibility for their own decisions and their own lives. Fast food companies are blamed for childhood obesity, rather than the decision-maker who lets the child eat this food. Companies are sued for safety breaches caused by workers who thought it wasn't cool to wear their safety harness. Smokers blame tobacco companies for their health issues.

The victim directs their attention towards the perceived threat, but they've picked the wrong target. And this is why they experience the same pattern of indignities and injustices throughout life. When you try to change your life by targeting the wrong cause, it changes nothing. When you target the real cause, you can create the life you want.

› the true victims

People suffer difficult circumstances all the time. We talk about victims of crime, victims of natural disasters, victims of terrorism, victims at the hand of another. Our language reinforces the belief that where there is a victim there must be a perpetrator, even if the perpetrator is nature herself. It's interesting how media coverage of floods is peppered with terms like 'the angry river' and 'intent on wreaking havoc' as if nature has intended to disrupt human life. Messages like this encourage people to look outward for the source of blame and fault. But this path only serves to strengthen the victim mentality and leads further away from happiness.

There are many examples of people who have been affected by a situation but who have chosen *not* to become a victim. We often call them heroes. Peter Hughes survived the 2002 Bali bombings. He was enjoying a night out with his mates at the Sari Club in Kuta when a suicide bomber changed their lives. Peter survived with burns to 60 per cent of his body, but many people died, including six of Peter's mates. Peter was in a coma for a month, went through a long painful recovery from his burns, and was told he would not work again. But Peter did not accept this grim outlook. He built his roof-tiling company into a multimillion dollar business and started the Peter Hughes Burn Foundation, helping hundreds of people survive and thrive after their own burn experiences. Peter was a victim of terrorism, but he refused to adopt the victim mentality. He said 'It's no different to someone who's gone through cancer, or the trauma of a car accident, or even a marriage break-up—it's how you come out of it. I'm one of the lucky ones. The benefits of what happened to me are because I haven't taken the negative line on anything. I'm not bitter, I don't blame anyone, I've got no anger.'[22]

Victims become heroes by seeing a situation as it really is, and taking responsibility for how they respond. Yes, this thing happened, but now I have a choice. I can succumb to the role of the victim and remain powerless, or I can take steps to find a new place in my changed world.

Why, when we can point to countless examples of inspiring people who are resilient in the face of tragedy, is it increasingly common to hear the whining voice of the victim in common everyday situations? Why does one person get on with life while another stops in his or her tracks, weeping and moaning? We need to look once more to the human brain to find some answers. It's all about fairness, avoidance and addiction.

› that's just unfair

Have you ever felt the urge to stand up for the underdog or fight an injustice? Do you ever hear yourself say or think 'That's not fair!' or 'That's just so wrong.' The human brain is highly attuned to detecting unfairness. Research shows that your brain responds to unfairness, injustice, offence or disadvantage in the same way that it responds to physical pain or discomfort. Studies on fairness usually consist of an ultimatum game, where two people are required to split a sum of money between them. The first person proposes how to split the money. The other person then chooses whether to accept it. If the offer is accepted, the money is distributed in that proportion. If it's rejected, no-one receives money. Subjects typically reject offers that are less than 20 to 30 per cent of the stake.[23]

In 2003 the ultimatum game was taken one step further and played by subjects whose brains were being scanned during the game. Participants played ten rounds, each with a different partner. Half the offers were fair and half were significantly less than a 50/50 split and deemed unfair. Scans revealed that participants' brains produced activity in the pain centres when an unfair offer was proposed. It was clear that social pain was interpreted in the brain in the same way as physical pain. When you are not treated in a way that is fair and just, it is literally like being physically assaulted.[24]

It's normal to look for ways to avoid pain and many of your brain's fears are designed to make you do just that. The victim mentality emerges from another one of these fears: the fear of facing the truth. The truth isn't always pretty and it can carry the sting of social pain.

Teresa is a lawyer and she is very proud of her professional reputation. She works hard and her bosses rely on her thorough research and detailed eye. One day she met us for drinks after work, and she appeared looking stressed and anxious. She was mortified about what had happened at an important meeting with a client a few days before. Her boss had delivered a presentation that suggested a very specific course of action, but the client seemed perplexed. 'What have you based these assumptions on?' he asked. Teresa pulled out the paperwork she had prepared. 'That figure there is not right. It's missing two zeros' the client pointed out. Teresa said the room fell silent, and she could feel all eyes turn to her. 'And in that moment I just didn't know what to say.' But her boss jumped in, apologised profusely to the client, and committed to sorting it out overnight. As she walked out of the building with her boss, Teresa still couldn't speak. Her boss just turned to her and said 'What happened?' Teresa told us 'I was torn between saying it wasn't my fault because I got the data from one of the client's people, or just accepting that I should have seen that the data didn't make sense.'

› i didn't do it

Accepting blame can be threatening. In most cases there will be consequences, and your brain shifts into high alert looking for a way to protect you. Studies show that by the age of four, almost all kids will start experimenting with lying to avoid punishment.[25] In their coming years they will use it to increase their power, manipulate friends, get attention, and fool their parents. While most have the habit socialised out of them by about seven years of age, the tendency to use denial to avoid negative consequences and social pain still remains in our armoury, and we all use it from time to time. Teresa was very tempted to go there when her boss demanded an explanation. But we were very proud to hear that Teresa had the courage to take responsibility for the situation. She knew that being a victim would get her nowhere, and most likely disappoint her boss even further. She said 'I know I learnt a lot from this situation and I was really surprised by how supportive everyone was and how they helped me to do all the rework. But I'm exhausted, and I hope I never do something like that again!'

If you proceed through life strengthening the technique of denial, your brain embraces it as a preferred response in any situation where negative consequences loom. You start to believe that the defensive position ('It wasn't my fault') deflects accusing eyes and pointing fingers. But it doesn't, it's just a way to ignore them. If I blame someone else for my child's obesity, I don't have to face the fact that I have failed as a parent. If I blame the tobacco company for my disease, I can avoid facing some poor choices in my life. If I blame my employer for my injury, I can deny that it was my own decision not to do the right thing.

Refusing to face the truth and deal with the consequences of any situation will not make it go away. In fact, the delay can make it harder to deal with as time goes on.

∨ ∨ ∨ ∨ ∨

› Over coffee with Amanda after the school reunion, she gave me the run-down on her life. Like many victims of divorce, she was struggling to move on. It was a 'no fault' divorce and the breakdown of her marriage left her feeling sad, angry and confused. While these are not unusual emotions considering the circumstances, it had been five years since the divorce and her emotions had become increasingly more destructive. She had lost a number of boyfriends, two jobs, and many old friends who were sick of hearing her story over and over again. I noticed she had a permanent tone of self-righteous indignation in her voice and had developed an argumentative style that emerged quickly in any situation. She found fault with the staff and the coffee at the cafe where we met, and her stories revealed that she also took issue with her neighbours, her new employer, and even her own accountant. But when I asked Amanda if she was happy she said, with indignation, 'Of course I am. I'm much better off without him. I'm over it.'

∧ ∧ ∧ ∧ ∧

› misery loves company

Habits are addictive. We've explored why repetition strengthens your brain's neural pathways, and makes it easier over time to slip into a habit without even thinking. Amanda's brain was doing this, finding fault now in everything and everyone. She was now addicted to the habit.

When you hear the term addiction you usually think drugs, alcohol, or maybe chocolate! But you can get addicted to the effect that your own thoughts and emotions have on your brain and your body. Your brain floods your body with chemicals all the time. They are the messengers that tell your body how to respond to a situation. In fact these chemicals are the reason you experience emotions as feelings. Certain neurotransmitters are involved in triggering a feeling of wellbeing and reward.

Whenever you experience a positive response to a behaviour, your reward centres are flooded with these chemicals. Drugs of abuse recruit the same brain mechanisms. Just as these can become addictive, so too can rewarded habits. So what if you have been winning the attention of other people through negative habits? Just one 'You poor thing' from a friend can reinforce the victim, by lighting up the reward centres of their brain.

ˇ   ˇ   ˇ   ˇ   ˇ

› Amanda's sister had been her closest confidante and support since her divorce. She too had experienced the pain of breaking up, and it hadn't gone well. She had taken Amanda's side without question, and she could be relied on to respond any time Amanda reached out. She would mirror Amanda's indignation 'Of course you deserve better!' What she did not realise was that her support was giving Amanda's brain a burst of positive reinforcement every time she played the victim role. This was one of the major reasons why, five years down the track, Amanda still had not found a way to move past this event and build a new life.

ᴧ   ᴧ   ᴧ   ᴧ   ᴧ

You don't have to like something to become addicted to it. The brain does not distinguish between what is good for you and what is bad for you. It just strengthens the habits you reinforce. Amanda's brain kept looking for the stimulation that sympathy and validation gave to her reward centres, in the same way that a drug addict seeks their next fix.

The pattern of the victim mentality is complex. It can start as a technique to avoid pain, but end up as a particularly harmful addiction. As the habit grows, you become increasingly negative but strangely satisfied by the emotions you feel when you focus on finding fault and complaining. From this place, it is impossible to make the changes you need in your life. A victim truly believes that finding fault in others protects them from the threat of facing something painful. So every act of blame or whinging triggers the reward centres: well done, you're safe!

› facing up and bouncing back

When J K Rowling wrote her Harry Potter series of books, her manuscript was rejected by 12 publishing houses, before a small group decided to take her on. It became the bestselling book series in history, and J K Rowling is one of the richest women in the United Kingdom. If she had been a person with a victim mentality, she would have faltered in the face of the first rejection. While those with a fear of failure feel demoralised or embarrassed when something does not work out, because they feel that it is their fault, those with a fear of facing the truth feel bitter and resentful, because they feel it is *not* their fault.

The negative patterns of thinking that are the hallmark of the victim become self-fulfilling prophesies: 'See, I told you things never work out for me.' Victims give up when the going gets tough. They lack resilience, an essential skill that can be found in the armoury of all successful, fulfilled and happy people. Resilience is the ability to navigate through adversity and bounce back. The first step to resilience is being willing and able to face the truth, then accept what you find there. The second step is taking responsibility for how you respond.

You may remember a book and subsequent movie, *Touching the Void*. It told the story of two mountaineers, Joe Simpson and Simon Yates, and their near-fatal climb of the 20,813 ft Siula Grande in the Peruvian Andes in 1985. Many teams had previously attempted and failed to climb the face, but Joe and Simon were successful. But the ascent is only half the challenge in mountain climbing. On their way back down, Simpson broke his right leg. In a disastrous chain of events, he then fell 150 ft into a deep crevasse. Yates assumed he was dead so had no choice but to descend the mountain alone. But Simpson had survived the fall. He finally faced the reality that if he was going to survive, he would have to save himself. With severe injuries, no food or water, and almost delirious, he spent three days crawling his way to base camp.

In interviews, he said that he remembered thinking 'It's just not physically possible' to get back to base camp. He said he couldn't deal with the big picture so he broke everything down into small targets. 'I've got to get to the cliff in 20 minutes.' And that's how he made it back. By facing one small reality at a time, taking responsibility, and applying himself to the task, he displayed the mindset that allows someone to rise above difficult circumstances and take control of their own destiny. Even if he had not made it back, the commitment to trying was a more powerful statement than simply giving up.

Survival is often all in the mind. Simpson went on to be told by doctors that he would never climb again, but after two years of rehabilitation, he was back on the mountain. In contrast, a victim does not overcome setbacks, because they don't even try.

› victims waste time and energy

People who adopt the victim mentality waste a lot of time and energy, focusing on the target of their blame or avoiding facing the truth. In the time they have spent complaining about something, they could have actually dealt with it. When you take responsibility for yourself, you spend less time agonising and dwelling on things and more time just doing them.

Liam is an accomplished guy in many ways, but at work he seems to have a chip on his shoulder. He says all the right things about good leadership and how to perform well, but he also has an 'I know it all' attitude. It drives his boss crazy. Any attempts to crack his shell or get him involved in development opportunities are met with resistance and avoidance. Liam has been encouraged to attend a few development programs, but has always found a way to get out of them. It's clear that Liam cannot see past his view that he is fine, and it's everyone else who needs to improve.

Finally, Liam was cornered and he had to go to a two-day program. His response to every opportunity to develop a skill or identify an opportunity for improvement was 'No, there's nothing I need to do there. Well, maybe something about getting my staff to be more productive.' He turned everything around to be about others, and left the program as much a victim as when he arrived.

Not only was Liam expending a lot of energy in his efforts to avoid facing up to the need to improve his skills and lose his attitude, he was setting himself up for a career crisis, as it became clearer to his boss that there was no way to get Liam to face reality. He wasn't as good as he thought he was; but he really could be if only he would only take responsibility for himself and stop running from the truth.

› victims become isolated

The negative patterns of the victim are hard for others to be around. A casual conversation can suddenly turn into an emotional diatribe and this is exhausting for the listener. There's nothing worse than being stuck with the victim at a party. 'How are you?' is interpreted as an invitation to update you with the latest round of injustices. You try to steer the conversation to more positive topics, or even propose a different perspective on one of the victim's current blockages, but your words fall on deaf ears. The mind of the victim is stuck on a particular pathway and, if the information you put in front of them is in conflict with the way their mind sees the world, it is rejected. This is how the brain works.

So over time people start to avoid the victim, not only because they are exhausting to be around, but also because it is clear that they cannot be shifted. They are often given up as a lost cause. Unfortunately they read this increasing distance from their friends through the victim mindset: 'What's their problem? Are they too important to hang out with me now? They are so selfish. They never supported me anyway.'

› victims repeat past patterns

Einstein said that the definition of insanity is 'doing the same thing over and over again and expecting different results.' I worked with Tony many years ago and we've stayed in touch. He is an engineer with a fair bit of experience who has jumped around many big firms where his skills have been keenly sought. But he never stays long and he always has the same excuse about why it hasn't worked out. 'They just don't listen to me.' He feels that his expertise is being ignored and they don't deserve to have him. So he goes to the next company, where they sound like they will appreciate him more. But the pattern repeats itself and Tony just says 'They're all the same. None of them know what they're doing.' Tony can't see that he has a chip on his shoulder and that his experience is worth little to a company if he can't contribute effectively in the team. Tony has recently decided to retire, but it's sad to see that he never really achieved his goals. He blames 'them' and cannot see that there was anything he could have done differently to change his path through life.

The sad thing for victims is, they are so busy focusing on the perceived threat, they simply cannot see that they may have contributed to their situation. We're not saying that a victim of crime or natural disaster or any other unfortunate event was somehow responsible for what happened to them. All of us face circumstances outside of our control. But the greatest threat to your happiness is how you respond to these situations, not whether they happen. Would you keep going back to the same restaurant over and over again if the food was bad, the service poor and the price outrageous? Hopefully, you would not give it too many chances before you face the truth that you can't change the restaurant, but you can change your choices and not return again.

› victims live in the past

v v v v

› Amanda was living in the past. She acted as if her ex-husband was still watching, and as if her actions were exacting some sort of revenge. But no-one was watching and her actions were only hurting herself. If she had been able to face this truth many years ago, and put her energies into creating a new life on her own, she would be in a different place by now. Victims become paralysed, because they direct so much attention towards keeping a watchful eye on their perceived threat, everything else in their life grinds to a halt. Opportunities are pushed away with suspicion; positive comments are received with cynicism; negativity becomes the default response; and a person's whole life can be consumed by finding evidence to support their position.

^ ^ ^ ^ ^

The brain wiring of the victim can be the most destructive pattern for anyone to hold, because it masks all the other fears. Unlike those other fears, the pathways are particularly designed to direct your attention away from yourself. The very thought of looking inside for the cause of your pain is impossible to comprehend. Most victims will push back very hard if someone points out that maybe they are creating their own unhappiness.

› being in control of your destiny

Some know Martha Stewart as the goddess of domestic perfection. She is an entrepreneur, author, publisher and television personality, who has achieved worldwide success. But she has hit some roadblocks along the way. In 2004, she served five months in jail, after being convicted for lying to investigators about a stock sale. There was great speculation that it would be the end of her career; but she came back stronger than ever in 2005. Within 12 months, she returned her company to profitability and launched the popular *Martha Stewart Show*. In 2011, she was inducted into the *New Jersey Hall of Fame*.

A very public jail sentence would be enough to make most people crawl into a hole and disappear from public life for good. Many assumed that her public profile was damaged beyond repair. But she turned things around and thrived. This only happens when you take responsibility for your life, your choices and your destiny.

When you let external events and circumstances dictate your life, you are like a small boat in a turbulent sea. One day you will feel the depths of despair, and the next day the thrill of a lifetime. But if you want to steer more smoothly through your life, it's time to face the truth that you are the captain of the ship, and only you can determine which way you turn in the face of the rising waves. Once you take responsibility for those choices and their outcome, you start to learn and grow, leaving negativity and blame behind in your wake. You have no time for those things. Life is too short to dwell on what did or did not happen and who did or did not do it. When you have the courage to face the truth and accept reality in all its gore and glory, you give yourself a fighting chance of finally creating the life you want.

> how to get wired for life

> happy new mind

Consider this for a moment. It's New Year's Eve and you are reflecting on how long it has been since you played a sport. You decide, as a New Year resolution, to dig out your old tennis shoes, get back on the court and win a tennis tournament. The tournament is only six months away. So how do you prepare? Will you put it out of your mind until the day before, or will you start a training regime? If you have any chance of winning, hopefully you choose the latter option.

Undoubtedly, your training regime would be made up of a combination of exercises. First, you would need to get off the couch and get fit! Some form of cardio work-out would be essential, before you could even step out on the court and make it through a full set. Let's throw in a 5km run four times a week. You would also benefit from strengthening the key muscles used in tennis. A gym circuit every second day, focusing on your shoulder and arm muscles, would start refining your body into a tennis playing machine. Finally, it would be hard to win without honing your technique and polishing up your serve, volley and backhand. A weekly session with a tennis coach should do the trick. After practising these three different forms of exercise over the six month period, you would surely be in a great position to achieve your goal.

It's a pretty logical formula, and few would deny that a training regime like this would be essential to achieve this goal. We've been bombarded with education about our physical health and fitness for years.

The activity at your local gym provides evidence of how well understood the benefits of physical exercise really are. People flock to all sorts of aerobics classes and cardio machines after work, hit the weights room, and hire personal trainers to focus on a particular area of their body. They don't only do it when they have a problem. They keep doing it to maintain their health and fitness. We know that we can't get there without regular exercise, and we can't maintain it if we stop.

So why do you think you can achieve the life you want, without a similar training regime for your mind? The truth is you can't. A program to train your mind is what's needed to overcome the mindsets that hold you back and to get wired for life.

› the mind fitness revolution

When you went to school, you probably participated in PE (physical education). You would have played sport and learnt the value of physical exercise. But it is most unlikely you also had classes on ME (mental education) and the value of exercising your mind. Where was the class that taught you the mindsets for success, how to be happy, and the skills for navigating the challenges that life throws us?

Even professionals, who you would expect to take the lead in mental education, are slow off the mark. In 2007, Dr Daniel Siegel, a prominent researcher and educator on the mind said: 'After asking over 65,000 mental health professionals face-to-face in lecture halls around the world if they had ever had a course on the mind, or on mental *health* (as distinct from mental illness), 95 per cent replied "no".'

Over the last ten years, we've watched the dawning of a new way of thinking. The idea that it is possible to rewire the mind is gathering momentum, and bringing with it the hope for a better way to live. Prominent neuroscience professor Dr Richard Davidson pioneered studies that proved the benefits of training the mind. His experiments revealed that you can become happier and more compassionate, in the same way that you can become better at tennis.

Your children, grandchildren, nieces and nephews are the first generation to benefit from a mind fitness revolution. The burgeoning knowledge on the brain, how it really works, and the fact it can be moulded and changed, will drive one of the greatest changes that you might ever witness. Human behaviour is being demystified. The pathway to a better life is being simplified. And the power to be the person you want to be is being clearly placed in your own hands.

We can picture a world, not too distant, in which fitness of mind will become as much a part of life as fitness of body. It will be well-recognised that fitness of mind is something that can be enhanced through exercise, and will be lost through laziness. It will be understood that you can feed your mind things that are good for it or things that are bad for it, and you will feel the effects accordingly. It will be acknowledged that you can reshape your mind to achieve real changes in your life, and that there is a method for doing so.

› wake up, think differently, and grow – the *mind gardener method*

Do you remember that you are a mind gardener? We mention it again because you might have forgotten. And it is one of the most important realisations you can ever have: that *everything* you think, learn, see and do shapes your brain and changes your life.

The life you have now is a direct result of everything you currently do to cultivate your mind. Whether consciously or unconsciously, you are planting the seeds and watering the weeds, and your life has no choice but to grow in the direction of your thoughts. If you want to get wired for life, there's no time to waste. The fears that flourish in your mind when your brain is left to its own devices can be conquered, but only when you commit to your mind gardening efforts and make every thought count.

Your brain is plastic and you are only limited by your own awareness, your desire to change, and your willingness to take the steps. It's time to wake up to the fascinating activity of your mind, recognise that you are the architect of your thoughts, emotions and actions, and that, by cultivating your mind intentionally and wisely, you can grow in ways that will change your life.

There are three distinct and important ways of exercising your mind. While each offers particular benefits on its own, it is the combination of the three types of exercises that delivers real and sustained changes to your mind and to your life.

> wake up - *the first step for rewiring the mind*

Your own way of living and operating has become second nature, but this just means your brain is often on autopilot. Habits are repeated without thinking and, frankly, in this mindless state, you are absolving all responsibility for your actions and allowing your brain to take the driver's seat. When you are on autopilot, your instinctive fears and learned habits are the map by which your brain navigates. But when you switch the autopilot off and switch your mind back on, you can design your own map and 'the world is your oyster'.

Waking up is a dying art. It is the first thing you must revive, if you really want to change your life. Wake up to the world around you, and wake up to your internal world. Because only when you are alert, switched on, focused and present, will you find yourself in the position to truly choose a different path. Nothing else but your own heightened awareness will enable you to see when you stand at the crossroads and face a moment of choice, that will either let your habits of mind rule your life, or release you from their grasp.

> modern-day mindfulness - aerobic exercise for your mind

Have you noticed how often you see and hear the word mindfulness these days? No longer relegated to alternative therapies and eastern philosophies, mindfulness is rightly moving into the mainstream. As studies on mindfulness reveal its full impact on the brain, on emotions, and on behaviour, it is fast being recognised as the essential life skill that has been underestimated for too long. Mindfulness switches on your brain and turns off the autopilot. And the good news is that mindfulness is a simple skill that can be learnt and practised anywhere, at any time. You don't need a meditation cushion or a quiet space, and you don't need to subscribe to any form of philosophy or lifestyle.

We all experience degrees of mindfulness. You can be mindful of other people, making sure not to bump them as you move through a crowd. You can be mindful of the building sense of excitement at a rock concert. You can be mindful of your own frustration in certain situations, and know that you are being unreasonable. Or you can be mindful of your mind itself, seeing your fears or mindsets as they arise, and recognising the point at which they start driving your emotions and actions. It is this deep quality of mindfulness that wakes you up and prepares your mind to think differently.

Mindfulness is the skill of paying attention, becoming aware of both your external surroundings and your inner activity of mind. When you are mindful, you are an observer of all that is passing by. You notice sounds, sights, smells, tastes and touch and your brain receives this rich information in its natural state. But, more importantly, you notice what your mind is doing with this information. You notice that a particular sound has captured your attention, and that you are drifting off into a memory that has been triggered by this sound. And noticing this, you can make a choice to direct your attention back into the present, or stay with the memory if you wish.

Mindfulness is like aerobic exercise for the mind, because it is designed to improve your mental stability, enhance your awareness and enable you to better focus your attention. When you are in a mindful state, it becomes easier to learn, change and grow. Rather than working hard to break habits of mind and form new ones, mindfulness literally prepares your brain for suspending its automatic responses and habitual patterns. Just as great aerobic fitness makes completing a tennis match more like fun than hard work, a healthy level of mindfulness makes it easier to navigate life's challenges.

Mindfulness exercises wake you up and, over time, waking up becomes a habit of mind. You can practise mindfulness exercises anywhere and any time. While meditation might be the best known mindfulness practice, you could compare meditation with a gym work-out. When you do a sitting meditation for 20 minutes, it builds up your reserves of mindfulness, just like running on the treadmill for 20 minutes will build up your aerobic fitness. But 'modern day mindfulness' is also about paying attention throughout the day, using all your normal day-to-day activities as an opportunity to exercise your mind. Just as you might take the stairs instead of the elevator to add some aerobic exercise to your day, paying attention to a whole range of normal daily tasks boosts your mindfulness. Chapter 9 describes how to build the skill of mindfulness and the habit of waking up.

> why waking up can be difficult

The average person has more than 50,000 thoughts and 12,000 internal conversations spinning around inside their head every day. You're probably aware of very little of this mental chatter, until you stop and pay attention. But it's this very lack of noticing it that trips you up. Because when mental chatter goes unchallenged, fears and mindsets find it easy to tighten their grip.

Your brain is not naturally inclined to be awake and mindful. It maintains a watching brief on your surroundings, but it spends the majority of its time absorbed in your tasks and testing incoming information against existing patterns. Its job is to produce a map for you to follow. It will encourage you to follow the map that requires the least effort, usually the one that's the most well-worn. It's not until you start waking up to your surroundings, that you realise just how much information your brain filters out. Stop right now and notice how many sounds there really are around you. Your brain has been filtering out anything that's not particularly threatening, and focusing instead on playing with all the ideas that have been triggered by the words on this page.

In the same way that we all experience varying degrees of mindfulness throughout a day, we are also bound to experience varying degrees of mind*less*ness. Forgetting someone's name the moment after meeting them; tripping over the bag you put out in the hallway five minutes ago; nodding through your partner's story then being caught out when they ask 'Did you hear anything I just said?'; and being angry about something at work and taking it out on your children when you get home. Mindlessness takes over when you are lost in your thoughts and not paying attention.

Let's consider the most simple case of mindlessness in action. You are waiting at a pedestrian crossing, thinking about your last meeting and wondering why your boss cannot just give you the go-ahead on your proposal. Your mind is playing with all the possible reasons: he is not been honest with you; he wants to take the idea and use it himself; someone else has got to him. The people in front of you start crossing the road, so you step out too. Then suddenly, a horn sounds loudly and you pull back, head up, looking quickly towards the horn. You realise the light had not changed, the other people had just done a quick dash between cars. Your adrenaline is pumping, all thought of the meeting has vanished, and you are hyper aware of your surroundings. You've just been snapped out of mindlessness in a split second. In your mindless state, your brain took its signals from the other people crossing the road, and it kicked in with the pattern that says 'Now it's time to cross'. It was unable to notice any other important information, because you were utilising its precious resources dwelling on your meeting. Only the threat to your safety made your brain suddenly turn all its resources to where they should have been in the first place: your surroundings, and making conscious and intentional choices about your actions. We see 'near miss' incidents like this all the time. People jogging with headphones on or texting while walking down the street, workers becoming complacent about their daily tasks and thinking about holidays instead. Mindlessness is spreading and it's time to wake up!

It's easy to blame the 'busy-ness' of your life for your state of mindlessness. There is no doubt that the barrage of information, the pressure to multitask, and the number of worries we seem to have in the modern world, all make it so much easier to slip into mindlessness. But let's be honest, mindlessness is a choice too, just like grabbing fast food instead of a healthy option. It is the biggest hurdle you face, if you truly want to get wired for life. Slipping into the comfort zone, operating on autopilot, and being complacent are all easy patterns for your mind to adopt. But it's like falling asleep at the wheel. Every time you forget that you are a mind gardener and do not choose to cultivate your mind, autopilot is your choice and your existing maps are your direction. Don't wait for an event in your surroundings to wake you up. Make every moment a mindful moment and you will reap the rewards.

› the side effects of mindfulness

Considering mindfulness as the equivalent to aerobic exercise for the brain is supported by many studies on its benefits. Mindfulness is linked to new neuron growth, overall brain health, positive emotions, improvements in physical health and immunity, and improvements in decision-making, memory, creativity, and the quality of relationships. Just as a fit body can breathe clearly and pump blood strongly through its veins, a brain that is mindful becomes clear, open, and functions at its peak.

It's extraordinary, but it is estimated that your brain receives many billion pieces of information per second through your senses, but processes only the smallest proportion of these, (somewhere in the thousands of pieces). Mindfulness frees up more of your brain's resources and, as a result, can process more information. We've all been in a conversation with someone who seems distracted. They nod and grunt at the right times, but you know they have missed the point. You get the distinct impression they will forget the whole conversation, and you may as well not have bothered.

But a conversation with someone who is present is a whole different story. Their openness gives you the feeling of being listened to and truly heard. They notice not just your words, but also your body language, your emotions and your unspoken concerns. They give you the confidence that they have understood the issues and they will make the right decisions. Their mindfulness has given them access to the tools of their social brain, as well as all the information received through their five senses.

It is for this reason that mindfulness has also been linked to better decision-making and overall performance. Mindful people get caught up in less activity than mindless people. Being able to distinguish between what's really important and the noise of the day means they act when it will make a difference and allow other things to pass by. A mindless person, on the other hand, reacts to everything: running in circles, putting out fires, then wondering why none of it had an impact. We all know an overachiever who's exhausted, stressed, unhappy and, after all that effort, no better off than their peers.

Scanning the brains of people who are practising mindfulness reveals that their brain activity shifts when in this state. They show greater synchronisation across the brain, which is associated with enhanced creativity and adaptability; and increased activity in the left prefrontal cortex, which is associated with enhanced happiness and positive emotions.

Finally, mindfulness has health benefits. Studies show that practising mindfulness for just eight weeks can deliver a boost to your immunity and reduce your risk of catching the flu.[26] It also moderates stress, and ongoing studies are examining the potential benefits of mindfulness for reducing the risk of age-related brain diseases such as Alzheimer's.

It's worth adding that no studies yet have identified a negative side effect of mindfulness!

> think differently - *the second step for rewiring the mind*

This step lies at the very heart of rewiring your mind and changing your life. Waking up enables you to see your activity of mind and the impact it is having on your life. But unless you make fresh choices, your life patterns will repeat themselves over and over again. Thinking differently is your opportunity to choose how you will see the world, how you will respond to the things that happen to you, and how you will design the roadmap in your mind. No thoughts, fears or mindsets are immovable. Your goal is to adopt the ones that best support your journey through life.

We explored five common fears that emerge when your brain's natural protective mechanisms form default pathways. You will know if one of these fears raises its head at some point in your life, hindering your efforts to create the life you want. There are many other mindsets and habits that each one of us has developed throughout our lifetime. Some serve us well and some do not. Somewhere in your reflections, and with a practice of mindfulness in your life, a mindset that needs rewiring will become clear.

> mindset busting and building - weight training for the mind

With 100 billion neurons, there are more possible connections within your brain than there are stars in the night sky! Since before you were born, your brain has been working hard to connect your neurons into complex networks that help you make sense of the world. When you learn something, a new pathway is laid down. When you repeat something, you strengthen these pathways. And when you break a habit, you weaken pathways, offering the opportunity to replace them with something new.

Thinking differently involves exercises that build, strengthen or weaken the neural connections in your brain. This is why they are like weight training for your mind. Pumping energy between connections makes them stronger. So, beware which mindsets you cultivate, because they are strengthened every time you give them attention. If you regularly dwell on the thought 'I really don't like that Monday morning meeting', your initial dislike for this meeting can grow to a full-blown aversion, making you take all sorts of avoidance action every Monday.

Imagine someone who instead focuses on a more productive mindset: 'The Monday morning meeting can be frustrating, but it is a good opportunity to understand what everyone else is working on.' This person is strengthening the wiring that leads to more positive behaviours, such as showing interest in others, listening attentively, and finding out useful information.

Neuroplasticity tells us that the brain is always doing some form of wiring. When your day unfolds as expected, existing pathways are reinforced. When something new captures your attention, new pathways are added. And when something forces you to rethink your existing views, pathways are abandoned. Your brain has been performing this merry dance of change for your whole life. When you were young, it was an adventure and you embraced it all. But it did not take too long for your brain to get stuck in a rut.

› the comfort zone

Your learning process is a wonderful thing, but it hides a sneaky trap. Once you start wiring up for a certain point of view, any other perspective starts to fade into the background. The brain is naturally biased towards what it learns first, and it will stick to these pathways unless a suitably strong impetus forces it to consider another view. The saying: 'First impressions count' recognises this tendency of the brain. And it applies not just to the impressions we create of other people. If you had a bad experience on your first trip to Paris, it doesn't matter how many times you hear that it is one of the most beautiful cities in the world, you won't like it. Many people have had their reputation ruined because this bias in our minds means 'mud really does stick'. This tendency to attach to first impressions is so strong that your brain will ignore information that is inconsistent with its initial view, unless it is threatening or loudly compelling.

This is why rewiring the mind can be difficult. Learning new ideas and rewiring mindsets should technically just be a matter of identifying the new mindset you wish to adopt, then repeating it until the new wiring takes hold. But it is not that easy, because your brain continually returns to its existing patterns. Your helpful brain is trying to limit the amount of energy you need to expend on learning new things, by proposing that you take a known approach first. But unfortunately, this just makes it harder to change your perspective and think differently.

This resistance to new approaches, information, ideas and perspectives is played out every day in so many ways. In businesses, managers talk about staff resisting change. Relationships fall apart, because couples get stuck in a rut. People rush through their day like mice on a treadmill. But the truth is, we are all just diligently following the maps in our head. People don't resist change, they just stay with what they know until there is a compelling enough reason to let it go.

A study of scientists in the 1960s explored why changes to scientific paradigms seemed to happen in major waves. The acceptance and adoption of new theories took many years. Rather than moving forward in the style of evolution, it took something more like a revolution to overthrow an old paradigm. What the study revealed, was that scientists will not let go of their existing perspectives until the evidence that it is no longer correct is absolutely overwhelming; and even then they will look for ways to keep some elements of their existing views alive.[27]

We are not being obstinate when we do this. We just have no map other than the one in our heads, and everything is filtered through that map. So seeing something new, particularly when it defies our existing map, is almost impossible. When you hear someone speak about experiencing the Boxing Day tsunami in 2004, they will tell of being glued to the spot, watching the water being sucked out and struggling to understand what it meant. For someone who had never seen or heard of this phenomenon, there was no neural pathway that could make sense of it. By standing still, they were following the only pathway their brain could propose: watch until I've worked this out.

By far the most difficult challenge you will face, when attempting to rewire your mind, is to unlearn an existing mindset. If you fail to recognise the importance of this step and jump straight to building new mindsets, you are undermining your own efforts.

› the sign you need to lift some weights

When you are driven by mindsets, you do not see a situation simply for what it is. You see it coloured by all the things in your mind that are triggered by that situation. When you hear yourself saying things like 'it shouldn't be' or 'it ought to be'; when you feel frustration or irritation arise; when you feel like you are hitting your head against a brick wall; it's time to wake up. Your mindset is clashing with reality, and the truth is, reality always wins. This does not mean you need to abandon your values and beliefs, preferences or goals. But be prepared to suspend them, take a fresh look, and be open to thinking differently.

Destructive mindsets lead to negative outcomes. Diets fail because of the 'all or nothing' thinking that causes a person who makes one small slip to throw in the towel and eat a whole buffet. Relationships break up because of all the 'should' statements that make a person feel constantly criticised. Even positive mindsets can be destructive if they clash with the world as it really is. If you were to examine some of the negative situations that have happened in your life, you would find that beneath the surface lie mindsets that have hindered your perspective.

When you train your brain to think differently, lifting weights that strengthen some mindsets and redirecting energy to allow others to wither and die, you start a new healthy activity in your life. The habit of thinking differently will open new worlds for your mind. Chapter 10 will show you how.

› grow – *the third step for rewiring the mind*

A flourishing mind is one that remains fresh and flexible. New mindsets are easier to cultivate when they are supported with new knowledge and fresh ideas. When your brain is stimulated, it grows new neurons and forms new pathways that can open up a world of new directions. A crucial step in cultivating a healthy mind is to adopt a lifetime practice of stimulating your mind and nurturing its growth.

› new skills and knowledge – maintaining a healthy mind

If the mindful exercises involved in waking up are equivalent to aerobic activity, and the mindset exercises involved in thinking differently are equivalent to weight training, then the exercises involved in growing your mind are the specific sporting skill you want to improve, like golf. Being fit and having strong muscles does not necessarily make it easy to take to the golf course for the first time. Sometimes when you wake up and think differently, you realise that you also need new knowledge and skills, if you are to successfully create the life you want. So go out and get them!

In the 1960s, an advertising campaign in Australia encouraged people to throw their litter in the bin, not on the ground. It's easy to forget that something as obvious as not throwing rubbish out of the car window was once a new idea. When I visited Vietnam in the late 1990s, I realised how important this step of adding new knowledge and skills can be to changing mindsets. I was travelling by train, and during the trip we were delivered a meal. We happily ate the food and piled up all of the disposable containers ready for collection by the attendants. When they came around to collect the rubbish, they piled it up on the trays then threw it out the window! The Australians in the carriage gasped with shock. But then I remembered that it had taken a massive campaign to stop us doing the very same thing when I was a little girl. The step of feeding the mind new knowledge is sometimes the critical ingredient in helping it grow.

You can learn from everything and everyone around you. But because the brain acts more like a filter than a receiver, you often learn only those things that reinforce your existing view. Being closed to learning new things invites ignorance, and ignorance is the root cause of many ills in the world: poverty, war, disease. Acting from ignorance means acting blind. To grow your mind and get wired for life, it is essential to stimulate yourself with new information, learn new skills, and keep your mind fresh.

› the brain training movement

Millions of people have taken to exercising their brains. 'Neurobics' is the latest trend. Brain training has become analogous with puzzles, quizzes and mental challenges. Nintendo makes games for it, websites are dedicated to it, and my mother, a crossword fan all her life, has now added the daily Sudoku to her morning ritual. Much research on this type of brain training suggests that there is nothing wrong with it, but it tends to improve only the particular functions of the brain associated with the challenge. So if your preferred form of brain training is Sudoku, then you are probably getting really good at Sudoku. This makes sense, because you are strengthening the neural pathways associated with that task. But you are not necessarily stretching and stimulating your whole brain, and you are not encouraging it to grow in new ways.

Many people join this new wave of brain training because they hope to slow the decline of their brain. Atrophy is a concept we relate to the body, but it is also highly relevant when it comes to the brain. Put simply, use it or lose it. An unused muscle will waste away, and so will an unused part of the brain. You might have been really good at mathematics when you were at school, but without continual exercise and training, you could find yourself struggling to help your children with their homework.

As we age, we all start complaining 'My memory is not what it used to be' or 'My brain is getting foggy' or 'I'm starting to lose it.' We are told it's a normal part of ageing. But the truth is, it's a consequence of failing to exercise your mind. In the middle years of your life when you are busy raising a family and working hard, you probably stimulate your mind relatively well without really trying. A study at Columbia University[28] found that people with more education and more stimulating jobs are at a lower risk of developing Alzheimer's. So if you think 'I can't wait to retire and just switch off' then think again.

› for brain training to be life-changing

If you really want your brain training efforts to be life-changing, we suggest you use three techniques. All are worthwhile in adding to your life.

‹ grow in ways that support your new mindsets

› As you wake up and think differently, consider whether there is a gap in your knowledge or skills, something that could support your new direction and help you become the best you can be. Maybe you've woken up to your fear of failure and finally taken the leap of faith to start your own business. If you've never been in this position before, your mind will grow even more by seeking knowledge and learning different ways to create success.

‹ grow in ways that open your mind

› Exposing your mind to new and different things will stimulate it and keep it fresh. Some of the greatest ideas in history came from people who exposed their minds to knowledge from many different subject areas, and allowed their curiosity to roam free. Leonardo da Vinci is a great example. He was an artist, musician, scientist, engineer, anatomist, writer and much more. His genius emerged from marrying together diverse fields of knowledge, creating novel pathways in his mind and unique results from his hands. The melting pot of your mind can perform magic when you mix up the ingredients, so don't limit its diet to the usual selection. Life is a tasting plate with much to offer.

‹ **grow in ways that maintain basic brain functions**

› You rely on your brain every moment of every day. You can exercise the basic functions that help you enjoy your life, by stretching yourself just a little further all the time. Repetition *and* novelty are key. And because your brain is a part of your body, it benefits from physical exercise and a healthy lifestyle too. Many studies have shown that a combination of aerobic and strength exercises will produce beneficial differences in the parts of the brain associated with memory, learning, attention and planning. It is also essential for neurogenesis, the process by which new neurons are born. And don't forget your brain food! You are what you eat, and so is your brain.

Chapter 11 explores practical ways for you to stimulate your mind and create a habit of thriving.

› **how often do i need to train in the three levels?**

You can't start training for something the day before and expect to be successful overnight. It is often quoted that, to be a world expert in anything, you need 10,000 hours of practice. But your life will be enhanced by even the smallest amount of regular mind exercise. You don't need to be an Olympic athlete to enjoy a regular tennis match, and you don't need to be a master meditator to wake up and thrive.

It is useful to have a structure and routine to get yourself in the good habit of cultivating your mind. So here is the recommended formula for getting the most out of the *Mind Gardener Method*.

• Aim for 20 minutes intentional cultivation of your mind every day. It's a small investment to make in creating the life you want.

• The proportion of exercises should be 50 per cent Wake Up, 40 per cent Think Differently, 10 per cent Grow

- As much as possible, incorporate your exercises into the things that you already do in your day. We have some suggestions in the next few chapters.

The exercises are not very difficult. Like any new routine in your life, your biggest challenges will be remembering to do them, and resisting the pull of your old habits.

› stories of the three steps in action

The late Steve Jobs, co-founder of Apple, delivered a speech at a Stanford Graduation ceremony. It provided a deep insight into the thinking that made him the Harvard Business Review's 'World's Best Performing CEO.' You will see the three steps of the *Mind Gardener Method* clearly in his story. Firstly, Jobs believed that his experience with Zen meditation taught him to concentrate and ignore distractions. He believed in having a beginner's mind and seeing the world through new eyes. His mindfulness practice enabled him to see things clearly, and notice opportunities that others missed. He had cultivated the art of waking up.

Jobs also had a unique ability to step outside of the mindsets that seem to dominate the business world. This did not necessarily make him popular, but it did make him successful. He trusted his intuition and curiosity, and did not slip into the habitual assumptions that burden many business people. His intuition often took him from the well-worn path but he didn't let the need to conform or the fear of failure drive him back onto it. Steve Jobs really had cultivated the habit of thinking differently.

Finally, Jobs was passionate about exploring things that interested him, even if they bore no relationship to his field of study or work. He tells a story of dropping out of college but continuing to 'drop in' to classes. He went to the ones that interested him and stopped taking classes that didn't. He followed his curiosity and enrolled in a calligraphy class, purely because he had a passion to learn. He had no expectation of any practical application of this skill at the time. But ten years later, when designing the first Mac computer, the use of beautiful typography became one of its defining features, and a major influence on how computers were designed from that point onward.

Steve Jobs was not following a formula, but his mind's potential was unleashed by being committed to waking up, thinking differently and growing.

Years ago, I decided I really wanted to conquer public speaking. There were a few reasons why I believed I was not successful. First, I would work myself into a bundle of nerves. I didn't sleep well from the moment I found out I had to speak until it was all over. Thoughts circled in my head like 'What if I forget what I am going to say?' 'What if I'm not engaging?' 'Am I expert enough to be speaking on this topic?' I believed I was going to fail, and I reinforced this fear of failure by dwelling on that possibility over and over again. I had also never received training in public speaking skills, because I didn't really believe there was any science to it. To control my nerves, I would write out a speech and learn it off by heart. I would then deliver it, word by word in a robotic state. I was so caught up in my own head that I had no awareness of the audience, and I was always anxious to talk to someone afterwards to find out how it went.

Today, I am a very comfortable and effective public speaker, and I put this down to three factors. Firstly, when I have a speaking assignment there are only two times when I think about it: when I am preparing, and when I am delivering. And at those times I give it very focused attention. I stay awake to the task and do not let my mind drag me off into old patterns that simply waste valuable time.

Secondly, if I notice thoughts like 'I'm going to fail' I shift my attention towards my strengths and towards the needs of the audience. Focusing on these two positive things draws my attention away from my fears, and immediately makes me feel more confident and enthusiastic. Thinking differently shuts off my brain's threat response and turns on my brain's reward response. This makes all the difference.

Thirdly, I read a book and attended a course on public speaking. Instead of assuming I knew it all, I brushed up on the skills and learnt techniques such as the power of storytelling. These skills enhanced my confidence and have been instrumental in changing the way I think about public speaking. Now I embrace it, enjoy it and rarely feel the twinge of fear.

› it all sounds a bit too simple

This is a common reaction when we outline the method in our programs. People keep looking at us and waiting for the rest of it. But don't be fooled by the simplicity of the steps. They can be very difficult to apply, because of your brain's natural tendency to return to its old habits. When this happens, many people fall into the trap of trying harder, adding more complexity to the method and doing too much. Just because the challenges you face in life seem complex, it does not mean the solution must be.

We heard a lovely story from a couple of leaders who had been through our *Conscious Leadership* program recently. It showed that they really understood this principle. The organisation was dealing with a natural disaster, and everyone was called in to help with the response effort. In the thick of phone calls, hurried voices and running people, one of the leaders started to get stressed. It showed in his voice and he was starting to find it hard to know which decisions to make. The other leader, noticing that her colleague was losing it, simply reached out and touched his shoulder. He immediately understood, brought his mind back to the room, and started responding effectively again. Her touch was his wake up call. Once he woke up, he could see that the only problem he really faced was his scattering mind.

Are you ready to wake up, think differently and grow? Let's take the first step to see how the Mind Gardener Method can transform the way you live.

> wake up

> An Olympic swimmer is standing on the blocks, ready to compete and win her race. She is aware of the crowd cheering, the cool air on her skin, her feet gripping the edge of the block, and the black line on the bottom of the pool. Her muscles are taut and she is free of thought, as she waits only for the sound of the starter's gun. Moments such as these, packed with anticipation and the single focus of a goal, will draw your mind into the present. Sports people call it 'the zone'.

At some time in your life you have been fully awake, absolutely present, and completely mindful. It happens to us all at different times. In nature, or when visiting a new part of the world, when playing your favourite sport, when meeting someone totally engaging, in a special moment like your wedding, when playing with your children, or just walking down the street on a perfect day. But you don't have to manufacture a situation like this to wake up your mind. It is a skill and we're going to show you how to develop it.

› first, the myths and misconceptions
‹ mindfulness is a buddhist thing

› Being mindful is an ability that every human mind is born with. Without it, you simply could not pay attention to anything around you, notice your surroundings, or even notice how you feel. The only reason it is so strongly associated with Buddhism is that this group of people have recognised the value of mindfulness, and have developed ways to strengthen it. You can learn much from their experience, just like you can learn lots of great tips for improving your tennis from Roger Federer. But dismissing mindfulness, because it is often linked to the practices of Buddhist philosophy, is as crazy as dismissing pizza as a food option, because it is associated with Italians!

‹ being mindful means having no thoughts

› This common misconception causes many people to give up too early in their attempts to develop a mindfulness habit. With the best of intentions, people try mindfulness techniques like meditation or yoga knowing that they are beneficial. But their first experience might be challenging to say the least. Their busy mind just won't stop. In fact it just seems to get noisier, faster and more overwhelming. They might try a few more times, then give up saying 'I'm no good at this. I can't stop my mind!'

The thing you need to know is that having a quiet and still mind is not the goal. The true test of improvement in mindfulness is just like the true test of improved cardiac fitness – it's your recovery time. You know you are physically fit when your heartbeat returns to its resting rate quickly, no matter how much you puff and pant during your exercise. It's the same with mindfulness. It does not matter how many thoughts jump up and play around in your mind. The true test of mindfulness is how quickly you see that a thought has captured your attention and how quickly you then direct your attention back to the present. Your mind's primary job is to work with thoughts, so don't expect them to go away any time soon.

‹ It's just for stress reduction and relaxation

› Mindfulness is great for moderating stress and teaching you how to relax, because it counteracts the effects of a busy mind. But don't expect mindfulness to make you feel like you've switched off and are wandering around in a daydream. A mindfulness practice will leave you focused, clear-minded and invigorated. Stress levels drop, because your mind is not wasting vital energy playing with thoughts, fears and worries. Instead, it is directed with greater purpose. Stress reduction and relaxation are positive side effects of mindfulness, not the main game.

‹ surely it's okay to do a few things at a time

› You might think you are a multitasking master but you're fooling yourself; and you're creating a bad habit that will come back to haunt you. You might think you are completing a few tasks in parallel; but your attention is actually switching quickly between each task and back again. And every time you do that you lose the neural connections related to the previous task, as your brain goes looking for the relevant pathway for the next task. Studies suggest that when you multitask, it takes 1.5 times longer to finish everything, than if you complete each task before moving on to the next one.[29] And worse, you have been training your brain to jump around. Eventually you will find it difficult and uncomfortable to focus on just one thing for any reasonable period of time.

‹ how can i plan if i have to focus on the present?

› Now stop and think about this. When you plan, you look into the future and consider the things you need to get done. You might make a list, choose some goals and select timeframes for each task. You might even look back into the past, to see how long it took you last time you did the same tasks. But this activity is done here and now. You'll never finish your plan, if your attention drifts off. If you start reminiscing about the past, then find yourself looking back through old photos and forgetting that you were in the middle of preparing a plan, then the past has captured you. Consciously reflecting on the past and exploring possible futures are fine activities, if they are done for the cause of something you are focusing on in the present.

› how mindfulness really works

Your mind has a constantly flowing stream of attention. It is always turned on, but it is not always flowing where it is most needed. A person with a well-trained mind directs this stream of attention to the things that are important at any one time: the work in front of you, the person you are spending time with, the book you are reading, the street you are crossing. But more often than not, your stream of attention is splintered in many directions at once. You are cooking with a phone in one hand talking to your mum, the kids call out a question and you answer 'Wait, I'm on the phone.' And at a more subtle level your mind is also trying to remind you 'I'll have to find that book I need for tomorrow before I go to bed.' And it might be mumbling 'Where is John? He better not be late again tonight.' Suddenly, you find yourself snapping at everyone and banging the pots and pans around. If you have built up your mindfulness, you would suddenly notice how distracted your attention is, and you would switch it back onto one task and stay in the present.

Mindfulness can be broken down into 2 components:

> **one** Awareness – being able to observe your mind in real time, noticing what is capturing your attention and the impact it is having
> **two** Attention – being able to intentionally switch your attention from place to place, and direct it into the present

Before we go into more depth, read the little experiment outlined in this paragraph, then jump straight in and try it yourself. Close your eyes and bring to mind a memory of something pleasant. Rest with that memory for five seconds, then turn your attention to something you are looking forward to. Another five seconds, then turn your attention to your favourite place. After a final five seconds, turn your attention to the sensation of sitting where you are right now.

How did you go? It's a little easier when someone talks you through it as we do in our programs, but generally you would have been able to do this activity relatively easily. You may have struggled to land on a particular memory, or you may have jumped around a little, and possibly even wanted to stay with one of the thoughts that came up during the experiment. But it shows you the two components in action: you were able to observe what arose in your mind (eg. your favourite place), and you were able to switch your attention from one thought to the next, then back to the present.

Observing your mind can be a little like watching a movie. Images associated with thoughts come past, then they move on as the next one comes into view. The fact that you can move from one to the next shows that you can redirect the stream of your attention. But it might also have shown you that your stream of attention can get a little caught up, when it finds something it likes to play with!

› exercises to strengthen awareness

Just as you can see yourself pick up a glass, you really can see your thoughts and even your emotions. Part of your mind acts as an Observer, and the more you get it working, the stronger and more watchful the Observer becomes. But often during the day, your attention just drifts off and you don't realise how far away it has wandered. This happens because the Observer has switched off and stopped watching. You are once again asleep, following the map of your habits and mindsets. The purpose of training your awareness is to switch on the Observer as often as possible, so you can see where your attention is being directed or when it is captured by one of your fears or mindsets. Over time, your brain becomes wired to operate with the Observer remaining watchful.

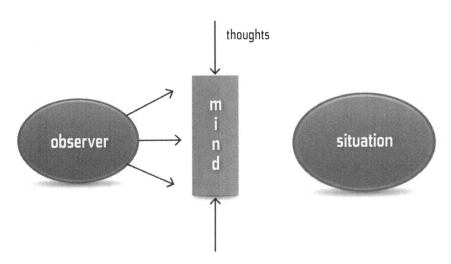

Start by asking yourself 'Where is my attention right now?' This simple question will trigger your Observer to switch itself on. And you will find you are either focused clearly on the task in front of you, or you are daydreaming, or something specific has captured your attention. As I write this paragraph at 10.20am and ask myself this question, I realise my attention is captured by the thought that I'd love a cup of tea and piece of cake!

Initially, you may find it difficult to really know what your mind had been playing with; but this is not important. At this stage, you are simply training your mind to switch on the Observer. Like starting leg presses for the first time in the gym, don't expect to see results immediately. In fact, like the leg press, expect to feel a bit of discomfort and resistance for a while. It may seem odd to just stop and observe your mind, and you might be surprised by what you find it playing with. But avoid judgement or criticism. Simply observe.

The following exercises will help you to train your awareness and switch on the Observer:

- Twice every day, sit quietly and just watch your thoughts for 30 seconds. Watch them as if you are watching a movie. Don't get distracted by any of them, but simply observe them and let them go as the next scene of thoughts rolls on. Increase this time to one minute the following week, and gradually to five minutes over the coming month.

- On the hour every waking hour, ask yourself 'Where is my attention right now?' This will remind the Observer to get to work watching the mind. Move this up to every half-hour in the second week.

- Challenge yourself to see how long it is before you notice that your mind has drifted off from the task at hand.

- Listen to a piece of classical music, and every time you notice your mind drift away from the sound of the music, make a mark on your notepad. Then return to just listening, until the next thought arises.

Tips:

- If you feel that your mind is getting busier over time, don't worry. It's not. You are just noticing activity of mind that you were missing in the beginning.
- Don't go looking for things in your mind, just gently observe. The effort is in remembering to do the training. But once you do it, don't force it.
- Whatever you observe, don't play with it. Notice it, let it go, and then watch the next thought come past.
- In the beginning, you are more likely to notice physical sensations than thoughts, eg. a sore neck from sitting too long at the computer. You may also notice emotions like 'I am frustrated.' These are all good observations and the more you practise, the better the Observer will get at honing in on the actual thoughts that have led to that state. Just let your mind get familiar with the new habit.

As you stick with this training, you will find that your Observer starts coming on without you having to specifically call it to action. You will start seeing a series of thoughts. Instead of wondering 'How did I start thinking about chocolate cake when I was just having a discussion about our budget?', you will be able to trace the pathway that your mind has followed. And as your training continues, you will reach a point where you don't have to retrace your steps. Your Observer will watch your mind in real time, and you will be able to see your attention moving from one thing to the next.

You may find it useful to keep a journal and write down what you learn about your mind: how often it is in the past or the future; which things distract it more than others; which thoughts trigger strong emotions. You may notice that there are particular thoughts that will tend to capture your attention. Maybe you have an inner critic that continuously points out the things that aren't good enough. Maybe you have a situation in your life that you are studiously avoiding. If you have strongly identified with one of the five fears in our earlier chapters, see if you can observe when that fear rears its head. For example, your mind might react to situations like a victim: 'I can't believe this has happened to me!' or 'That would be right, they've done it again' or 'Why me?'

Rather than going with these thoughts and letting them lead you back to the same place again and again, just watch them pass, observe what triggered them and note the effect they have. Stay with the Observer and stay awake to your mind. This is the point of the exercises.

˅ ˅ ˅ ˅ ˅

› Even though Bill had been able to overcome his win/lose mentality and enjoy his sea change, when he switched on his Observer he noticed that many of his thoughts were tied up in looking for threats. He was surprised by how suspicious his mind was! It should not have come as a surprise, because a large portion of his life as a politician was spent looking for the next issue that was going to bite him. Even though he had made a radical career change, his mind had been trained to respond in this way. He saw thoughts like 'Is this going to be bad for me?', 'I had better watch that person' and 'Something is going to pull me down' surfacing on a daily basis. He could manufacture a whole drama from one of these ideas without any effort. As he became more proficient at waking up, he found the stories his mind wove were quite fascinating, but usually very poor predictions of reality. And he realised that he spent a lot of time focused on possible futures, rather than being present.

˄ ˄ ˄ ˄ ˄

› exercises to strengthen attention

This second component relates to your ability to switch your attention from one thing to another. Remember, your attention is like a constantly flowing stream. It is at its most powerful when it is directed clearly onto one thing. This training is all about strengthening your ability to switch your stream of attention from one place to another, and to particularly direct it into the present.

The reason it is important to have your attention in the present is that this is the only place where you can make a difference. You cannot change the past, and the future is not yet here. If your attention is not in the present, two things happen:

> **one** You miss what's right in front of you and do not see the opportunity to act; and

> **two** You respond to things from your habitual mindset, not from the true need of the situation.

When your attention is not fully in the present, you are not making the best choices or creating your best life.

So once your Observer identifies where your attention is, it's time to gather up the fragments and channel them to the present. This ability to switch your attention intentionally is strengthened by repetition. The goal here is **not** to **stay** in the present. It is to return your attention again and again to the present. It will not stay there very long at all, because your mind is so used to noticing distractions, playing with thoughts, triggering your mindsets, and operating on autopilot. But that does not matter. If you have a busy mind, this just means you have more opportunity to train your attention than the next person!

When you did the little experiment at the beginning of this chapter, you were asked to switch your attention between different memories, ideas and preferences. But the exercises for training your mind to become present are more specific.

> come to your senses

When you are connected to one of your senses, you are present. It's a simple idea but consider how true this is. When you are lost in your thoughts and mindless, you don't notice the taste of your food; you don't hear someone ask you a question; you don't see a friend waving at you from across the road; you don't smell the flowers as you walk up the path; and you don't feel the breeze on your skin when you're standing near the window. But suddenly, if one of those senses receives a strong enough input, your attention is snapped back into the present. 'Wow, those flowers smell amazing!' or 'I didn't realise how cold it was getting.' Your day is full of moments when one of your senses suddenly summons your attention, and for that moment you are present.

So exercising your attention is as simple as regularly connecting with one of your senses. Don't wait for your senses to put out the call. Be proactive, and train your brain into the good habit of seeking connection with the present. The following exercises will strengthen your ability to switch your attention. Over time, directing your flow of attention to the present will become a natural habit of mind.

- When you are brushing your teeth, pay attention through taste to the toothpaste in your mouth
- When you are washing the dishes, pay attention through touch to the dishes, as you pick them up and move them around
- When driving your car, pay attention through sight to the movement of other cars around you
- When you are eating your food, pay attention through taste to the changing flavours in each mouthful

- When you are rushing to an appointment, pay attention through touch to your feet as they move along the floor
- When you are reading, pay attention through sight to the words on the page
- When in conversation, pay attention through hearing by listening to the sound of the other person's voice.

There are many activities in your day that you can convert into a brain-training opportunity. Usually, mundane activities are the best opportunities to help you strengthen your mind, because you do them every day. They will give you plenty of opportunity to practise focusing on your senses and becoming present.

ˇ ˇ ˇ ˇ ˇ

› Jodie practised being present by focusing more attention on her baby, instead of worrying about what time it was and the next thing her baby needed to do. She gave more attention to what her baby *was* doing, instead of thinking about what she *should* have been doing. She found activities that normally frustrated her, like bathing her baby, became like a mini meditation. She focused on the sense of touch, and kept her mind with the sensation of the water and her baby's skin. She thought of nothing else and finally this activity became one of the most pleasurable in her day. She would normally come out of the bathroom frazzled, because she was thinking of all the things she needed to do before putting the baby to bed. But now she actually came out refreshed. It didn't take any more time, she simply changed her mind and that changed her whole experience.

^ ^ ^ ^ ^

Tips:

- Connecting with one of your senses is a gentle exercise. If you find yourself listening intently to all the noises and commenting on them, then you have see-sawed too far and your attention has been captured again.
- Never try to pull your attention away from where it is captured by having a battle with your mind eg. 'Why am I thinking of that? I shouldn't do that. Stop thinking of it!' This just adds another layer of 'busy-ness' to the mind. Switching attention is not a negotiation, it is a physical action, so just do it.
- Don't wait until you are doing something 'important' in your day to become present. It is best to exercise your mind with regular everyday activities.

> putting it all together

When you combine the exercises that switch on your Observer with the exercises that switch your attention to the present, you have a complete mindfulness routine. But keep it broken down into its components, until it becomes more natural. When you feel ready, add the following three activities to your day and see what difference they make.

‹ pause often

> Imagine if you didn't have to carry the 'busy-ness' of the day with you, and you could wipe the slate clean every few hours. We recommend a technique that can help you do just that. A mental pause on a regular basis, involves resting your attention for just a few seconds on one of your senses. It only needs to be for as long as one or two breaths. This simple act will turn on your Observer and bring you back to the present. Here are some suggestions of times when the pause really works well:

- Pause between tasks. It will clear your head of the thoughts associated with the last task, and bring your full resources to bear on the next one.
- Whenever the phone rings, pause and connect with your sense of hearing for two rings, then pick up the phone. Alternatively, touch the receiver for a moment before answering. This will draw your attention away from whatever else you were doing and ensure it is directed fully to the ensuing conversation.
- Pause whenever someone interrupts you, by feeling your feet on the floor for a few seconds, then give your full attention to the person interrupting you. This is a much more effective strategy than trying to juggle your task and the interruption at the same time. You really will get more done this way!
- Pause whenever you feel a thought or emotion arising that is likely to lead you down an unproductive path. You'll get to know your own habits of mind, and this will become easier over time.

ˇ ˇ ˇ ˇ ˇ

› Amanda used the pause to diffuse her anger. When she felt she was getting agitated, she simply took a deep breath and felt the sensation of her breath moving in and out of her body. This enabled her to let go of the negative emotion and see her situation more clearly. She found that the power of the emotion diminished every time she paused.

Sarah used the pause whenever she was required to speak in public. As soon as she got up in front of a group, she would spend three seconds grounding herself, by feeling her feet on the floor. She felt that this simple exercise focused her mind and calmed her down.

Jodie found the pause her most valuable tool. She paused before she got out of the car after a day's work, and it helped her leave the stress of the day behind and focus on her home life. With the many tasks involved in being a working mum, she found pausing between each activity slowed her mind down and made everything less overwhelming. She started to feel that her priorities were becoming more balanced.

∧ ∧ ∧ ∧ ∧

‹ mindful listening

› Because most people spend part of each day in interaction with others, listening is a perfect activity for training your mind. Mindful listening is listening with full attention, without distraction, and without internal comment or dialogue. Even if you've been told you are a great listener, you may not have listened this mindfully before. Most people listen to others with a fair degree of internal commentary, although you might not be aware of it. Your mind is often considering 'Do I agree or disagree with what you are saying?', 'I want to jump in and say X', 'I know what you are trying to say' or 'I've got a solution to your problem. This is how I can help you.' Mindful listening means simply directing your attention to your sense of hearing and allowing voices to be heard, almost like you are listening to the sounds of the waves rolling onto the beach.

Mindful listening is a great technique for waking up, when you are interacting with people you have formed strong ideas and opinions about. It helps you to set these aside and simply listen, being open to your present interactions, without filtering everything through the wiring you formed in past interactions. You never know what they might say this time! It is also very useful when you think something or someone is boring. This is when your mind likes to escape and play with other thoughts. But if you let your mind get away with that, you are just encouraging bad habits. Switch your attention back into the present, by listening mindfully and keeping your Observer switched on.

You can apply mindful listening to yourself as well. Listen to the sound of your own voice. You'll find it makes you more alert to what you say and how you say it. This is a great activity for difficult conversations, public speaking, or times when you need to deliver your message very succinctly.

v   v   v   v   v

› Bill had many thoughts and emotions circling in his body when he first sat down with Tom, the other shop owner who he thought was going to ruin his life. He had observed that this conflict with Tom was mostly in his head, so rather than blurting out all the things he had wanted to say to Tom for weeks, he simply listened with full attention. And he was glad he did. The stories he had made up in his head turned out to be incorrect. He may have missed this, if he had gone in with his usual behaviour of monopolising the conversation, shouting the other person down and not listening to what they were saying. He realised it was the first time in his life he had ever truly listened. And this new skill scored many extra points with his wife!

∧   ∧   ∧   ∧   ∧

Remember that you can't just direct your attention to your sense of hearing once and expect to listen mindfully for a whole conversation. Your mind will start reacting almost immediately. You will need to switch your attention again and again to the sound of the other person's voice, right to their last word, before you even think about responding.

‹ meditation

› Meditation is like a gym work-out, where you dedicate 20 minutes to intense aerobic exercise. There are a number of meditation techniques and many are pure mindfulness exercises that train the two components of awareness and attention. Some use the breath as the point of focus, in exactly the same way as you use your five senses. Like them, your breath is always moving through your body, so if you are aware of it, you must be present. Meditation involves directing your stream of attention to the point of focus, noticing when your mind has drifted away, then gently switching your attention back. During a 20-minute meditation you are likely to drift off hundreds, if not thousands of times. So imagine how much great exercise your brain is getting in switching on the Observer and switching your attention! If you want to boost your mindfulness practice, meditation is a great form of proactive exercise and will help to wire your mind into this new habit more quickly.

ˇ   ˇ   ˇ   ˇ   ˇ

› Brett had been regularly practising some simple mindful exercises since he attended our program. Now he recognised that he needed something more to help him harness his busy mind. The thought of attending a meditation class seemed daunting, so he decided he would simply start at home. He got up half an hour before the rest of the household woke and sat in a comfortable chair. He closed his eyes and focused on his breath, and every time he saw his mind wander he simply directed his attention back to his breath. The first day he could manage only five minutes, but after four weeks of being disciplined enough to give it another try every morning, he was meditating for 20 minutes a day.

^   ^   ^   ^   ^

› building a mindful day

To maximise your results, you might consider designing a mindfulness routine for your daily practice, like the one below.

1. Wake up and take a few deep breaths while you are still lying down. Call the Observer to action before you rise: 'How am I feeling? What's occupying my mind already today?' Observe for a few seconds, then set an intention for the day. As soon as you get out of bed, switch your attention into the present by feeling your feet on the floor.

2. Find a place where you can sit with your spine straight. Sit quietly for one minute (and add another minute each week), focusing on your breath. Every time you get distracted, return your attention to your breath.

3. Brush your teeth mindfully and, as you get dressed, feel each piece of clothing as you put it on.

4. Pause with your hand on the door handle, just feeling it for a few seconds before leaving the house. (I find this a life saver, because it will usually reveal that I have forgotten something!)

5. Practise mindful listening throughout the day, in as many conversations as possible.

6. Pause between major tasks.

7. Watch for frustration, irritation or other strong emotions. They are a trigger to pause and switch on the Observer. What is disrupting your mind? Let it go by directing your attention to one of your senses. Then you can deal with the issue with a clear mind.

8. Pause before you get out of the car, bus, tram, train or ferry and connect your attention to the present by feeling the door handle before entering your home. This will help you fully engage with the people in your house and switch off the mental activity of the day.

9. Use cooking or eating dinner as a mindfulness practice: it has sight, sound, smell, taste and touch.

10. Repeat number two before heading to bed for the night.

› the rhythm of learning

You can often start something new with great expectations. You look for the benefits quickly, and can get disillusioned if they aren't obvious. So this is what you might expect to experience, as you build your mindfulness practice.

In the same way that starting physical exercise can be painful and uncomfortable, this can also be the case with mindfulness. You are expecting your mind to move in different ways to its normal habits, and it will initially resist. At this stage in your exercise efforts, discipline is the key. Simply remembering to practise will be your biggest challenge, but don't beat yourself up when you forget. Just do it whenever it comes to mind. Help yourself out by placing some notes around your house to act as little reminders, or use the cards from our *Mind Gardener Guides* to build momentum, and slowly it will become more familiar.

Some people experience no real impact from their first mindfulness attempts, while some people find that the first few times they switch their attention into the present is pretty impressive. You may notice an extra glow in the day, even a sense of calm, and you may find that whatever you were dealing with becomes more effortless. But don't get complacent at this point and think 'I've got this nailed' and don't expect that every time will be so powerful. You will probably next face the experience of the hard slog, when you keep trying the exercises and seem to experience no real benefit or impact at all. This is when many people give up, or try too hard. Please don't do that. Just keep gently practising to switch on the Observer and switch your attention into the present. Don't make it more complicated and don't go looking for the 'right' experience. Let your brain adapt and learn this new wiring. Every learning process takes time, and this is no exception.

You will not necessarily notice the benefits accumulating, but one day you will look back and say 'I never would have reacted that way three months ago.' This might be the first time you realise that your training has made a difference. Again, celebrate that achievement but don't get complacent. Many people drop the regular discipline at this point, and only revert to mindfulness when they face something difficult. But the best way to prepare yourself for difficult times is to maintain discipline all the time. Remember that mindfulness, like physical fitness, is something you want for the rest of your life. So stick with it.

You will go through a series of ups and downs with your training. You may experience periods when you see benefits every day, and you can see yourself becoming more mindful. Then you will experience periods when you feel that you have plateaued. This is natural and you should not fight it. As your neurons grow new connections, your brain needs periods in which it consolidates this growth. During this time keep practicing, but don't lament the lack of obvious benefit. It's all still happening inside your mind. We also encourage you to mix up your exercises. Just as your body can reach a point where an exercise does not seem to make much difference, the brain likes variety. There are many different ways to practise mindfulness in your day. Our *Mind Gardener Guides* and programs will provide many ideas and much inspiration.

› so what's next?

Remember that Waking Up is the just first step in rewiring your mind and transforming your life. Without a mindfulness practice, you will find it difficult to see or change the habits of mind, fears or mindsets that trip you up on your journey through life. But once you wake up to the world around you and the activity in your own mind, you are sitting in the driver's seat and the power to change direction sits squarely in your own hands. Now it's time to Think Differently and get wired for life.

› think differently

› Waking up shines a light on your moment of choice. When you stand at a crossroad and realise that your next step can either take you back down the well-worn path or take you in a new direction, you are in the best position to change your life. In this chapter, we first explore the tools that help you choose the new path and stay on it. And then we'll look at some exercises that proactively lay new pathways. Because when you see your moment of choice, you don't want the new path to end just around the corner.

› becoming aware of your moment of choice

There is a popular parable that tells of a man walking down the street and falling into a hole. On the first day the man does not see the hole, falls in and takes a while to realise what's happened before he clambers out. On the second day he still does not see it, falls in again and climbs out wondering how that could happen again. On the third day he falls in again, and gets angry with himself for being so stupid. On the fourth day he pauses at the hole; walks around its edge, but still falls in. On the fifth day he crosses the road, keeping his eye on the hole, but falls into another one! And on the sixth day the man chooses to take a different road!

When you stop focusing on how you can change the situation, and instead recognise that *you* are the only variable that you can change, you are ready to step onto your new path.

Moments of choice don't just come once or twice in your life. They happen continuously. The moment you act on one, then another arises and another. Every moment of every day holds the promise of a fresh start. But the times when you see you are just about to make a crucial decision, that will strengthen an old mindset and set you back down a path you wish to leave behind, are the times when you need some resources at your disposal.

› attention is the key

Your own attention determines which neural pathways get used and which ones do not. When you pay attention to your fears, habits of mind and mindsets, they receive more energy and they are strengthened through repetition. When you want to loosen their hold, you must harness your stream of attention and switch it elsewhere. What you focus on grows, and what you ignore gets weaker. If you want to weaken the hold that your current mindsets have over your emotions and behaviours, switching and directing your attention elsewhere is the only skill to use.

In Chapter 9, we explored how you can switch your stream of attention and direct it where you want it. This is critical for the purpose of waking up, because it keeps your Observer switched on and enables you to see the way your mindsets play across your mind. Once you are awake, you become more able to see them arise in real time, and notice your moment of choice. But once you reach this point, the level of control you have over your attention becomes even more important.

> what you focus on grows and what you ignore weakens

It's absolutely crucial to realise that in your moment of choice, attention is the *only* tool at your disposal. The way you use it will determine if you head straight down the well-worn path and back into the familiar patterns of your life, or whether you think differently and head in a new direction.

And you will have to direct it again and again and again. Attention never stays in one place for long, because your brain does not work that way. It will become more stable and focused with practice, but the truth is that switching and directing your attention is a second by second thing. So don't think that, just because you've seen your moment of choice, directed your attention and acted, you can now go back to sleep. If you want to be wired for life, you'll need to stay alert and climb back into the driver's seat over and over again.

So let's look at five ways you can use your attention wisely, when faced with your moment of choice.

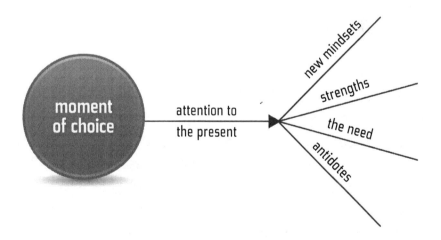

‹ direct attention to the present first

› Regardless of which other methods you adopt to help you focus your attention, you should always first ensure that your attention is in the present. When faced with a moment of choice, bringing your attention to the present will wake up all your senses. This pushes the pause button on your automatic default response. Your brain stops filtering everything through your mindsets, and instead starts wiring for whatever is actually happening right here and now. If you are walking down a dirt road, and fear is triggered by a coiled shape up ahead on the track, you are suddenly awake with all your senses drawn into the present by your threatened brain. This is automatic, but immediately, with your senses heightened, you can carefully assess the shape and see that it is actually vines fallen from a nearby tree. The fear is unnecessary and you can let it go.

It's the same with your habitual patterns of mind. They will arise, but if you are awake with your Observer switched on, you will see them. Being aware and present means you can now assess whether your mindset is filtering your perspective; does it need to be set aside, or is it a valid response to the situation?

Sometimes directing your attention to the present is enough. Imagine if you heard a comment by your partner, that triggered your fear of facing the truth, and you see yourself moving into victim mode. But being awake, before you react to anything, you make the choice to direct your attention to the present. And you realise that he was talking about something completely different, and you had misheard him.

Remember that your five senses will help you direct your attention to the present. Simply connect your mind to one of them, and your attention will move away from your thoughts and into the present. Keep it gentle and simple.

∨ ∨ ∨ ∨ ∨

› One day Brett saw a job advertised, that was more closely aligned to his passion. He worked up the courage to take the leap and apply for it, and was surprised to find he was short-listed for an interview. Brett recognised that he needed to be vigilant with his fear of failure. When he saw it in the days leading up to his interview, he simply acknowledged it and turned his attention to what he was doing at the time. If he saw the thoughts while he was eating dinner, he simply directed his attention away from the thoughts by really tasting his meal. Every time he did this, his fear of failure neural network was slightly weakened. He got through the days leading up to the interview, but he felt the nervous twitch while in the waiting room. He used the signal of the emotion as a prompt to let go of his mindset. He paused, taking a deep breath and felt his feet on the floor for ten seconds. His wiring was weakened again. As he went into the interview, he reminded himself to stay in the present, so those mindsets would not get attention. He did this by practising mindful listening. He listened to the sound of the interviewer's voice as she asked questions, and he listened to the sound of his own voice as he answered. By the time that experience was over, he was well down the path of unlearning his previous pattern of thinking.

Brett didn't get the job, but he didn't interpret it as a failure. The experience he had gained and the skills he had practised were a huge stepping stone, that he felt was taking him closer to his real dream.

∧ ∧ ∧ ∧ ∧

‹ direct attention to the need

› When you operate on autopilot, your brain responds to a situation through the filters of your fears, mindsets and habits of mind. Directing your attention to the present will turn autopilot off, and switch your clear and unbiased mind back on, if only for a few seconds. Maintaining this clarity can be supported by using key questions, to keep directing your attention away from your old habits of mind towards a more helpful perspective. Ask yourself:

- 'What is the real need in this situation, not *my* need?'
- 'What is my role here?'
- 'Is there a greater purpose that I am missing?'
- 'What is the most useful thing I can do right now?'
- 'Will this take me to where I want to be?'

The simple act of asking these questions helps to focus your attention on the situation in front of you, without your normal filters. In that cleared space, you are better able to see other ways of responding.

˅ ˅ ˅ ˅ ˅

› Sometimes it takes a bit of practice to catch yourself, and even more to make a different choice. Even though Sarah had become familiar with her fear, and understood the steps she needed to take to conquer it, she still faltered in the face of it, before she found the courage to stand out. She knocked back an opportunity to speak at a *Young Women's Breakfast*, but realised immediately that she had fallen into the same old trap. When a high-profile school approached her about painting the signature piece for their famous charity auction, she watched her fear rise as the Principal was speaking. But the pull was too strong, and she let her attention go with the fear and made an excuse about not having enough time to do it. After reflecting on how crazy this was, and knowing that she would need to take a leap of faith sooner or later, she called him back and accepted the amazing opportunity. The next time her fear arose was when a radio station rang, wanting to interview emerging artists. She again saw her fear in real time, but this time decided to ask herself one simple question 'Would the person I want to become accept this opportunity?' The answer was 'yes', so her answer was 'yes'. It didn't mean she wasn't nervous, but she was able to keep her attention with the need of the situation, and not with her fears. Her fears started to loosen their grip, and she excelled in the interview. Having a pleasurable experience and receiving praise made it even easier next time. To fear rejection was plainly unnecessary and she decided it would no longer rule her decisions.

^ ^ ^ ^ ^

‹ direct attention to your strengths

› Imagine you are doing a performance review at work, and you get some feedback from your boss. She tells you that you have been doing a great job at A, B and C but that your performance on D really hasn't been up to scratch. Which piece of feedback stays in your mind for the next hour, day or week? If you're like most of us, it will be the fact that you didn't perform on D! Losses hurt twice as much as gains feel good, and your brain directs its attention to the threat.[30] Improving D is important, but focusing all your time, thoughts and energy on it is nowhere near as effective as focusing on the things you are good at. What you focus on grows, so when you focus on your strengths, your overall performance and effectiveness flourish.

Focusing on your strengths probably isn't something that comes naturally. And you wouldn't be alone there. Studies on strengths reveal that 73 per cent of people use their strengths only once per week. Less than two out of ten people play to their strengths at work.

We've been reared in a world that focuses more on negatives, weaknesses and fears than it does on positives, strengths and courage. Up to 77 per cent of parents will focus on the subjects that a child is failing at school, rather than the ones in which they are performing well.[31] But focusing on strengths, and using them as often as possible, is associated with all positive measures of performance, happiness, wellbeing and community stability.

Here's how directing your attention to your strengths can work. When you face your moment of choice, and direct your attention to the present, sometimes the next step is not immediately obvious. So ask yourself any of these questions:

* 'What strength could I use here to move forward?'
* 'How could I apply my strengths in this situation?'
* 'If I used my strengths now, will it take me down a more positive path?'

ᵛ ᵛ ᵛ ᵛ ᵛ

› Amanda knew that her victim mentality was triggered in social situations. She always felt like people were judging her, and that she never really fitted in. She realised that acting the victim had become a defensive strategy, but it made her appear dismissive of people or critical of everything around her. One day, while watching the activity at an event from a quiet corner, she asked herself 'When do I feel most comfortable in social situations?' Immediately she knew that it was when people were talking about themselves, because she actually found other people's stories very interesting. Over the last few years, she'd lost the knack of asking people about themselves and just listening. Now she brings this to mind before she goes to any event. Whenever she becomes aware that she is starting to feel judged, she asks the other person a question about their own life. The different experiences she is having now are helping her to relearn the value of relationships, and to take responsibility for how people perceive her.

∧ ∧ ∧ ∧ ∧

If you're not sure what your strengths are, there are plenty of books, online resources and other tools to help you explore them. Look for things you enjoy, the times you feel most focused and engaged, when it is that you feel most competent, and responses that come naturally. What do people turn to you for? What role do you tend to play in a group? When you volunteer, what do you prefer to offer? Your strengths are innate characteristics that have always been in you. Ask family members and those who have known you well, what they think your strengths are.

The more you use your strengths, the stronger they will grow. Remember, repetition is the key for turning this new habit into a natural response.

‹ direct attention to a new mindset

› This is the foundation of thinking differently, and the place where your mind training truly creates the life you want. When you see your moment of choice, and you can direct your attention to a particular mindset consciously and intentionally, you are choosing your life. Habitual mindsets want your attention, but as new mindsets take root and grow, they offer an alternative. Every time you direct your attention to a new mindset, you nourish it and promote its growth. And because you are not nurturing the old pathways, they weaken and wither. Remember that old mindsets may never go away, but they will start to loosen their grip. And at some point, the new mindset might even become a default pathway, requiring less and less attention to activate.

While this strategy might sound like the most obvious one to adopt whenever you are trying to detach yourself from a mindset that is holding you back, it has traps. It will not work if you still feel some sense of belief in the old mindset. And it will not work if you don't really believe in the new mindset. It is only when you have had a true realisation that the way you think needs to change, that your neural pathways will let you in to start your work. But once you have, then the practice of continually switching your attention toward the new mindset is the only way to achieve sustained change.

We have suggested below how the mindsets associated with the five fears might look, and some more productive mindsets that could replace them. Once you recognise that the mindsets in the left hand column hold you back and need to change, you are ready to start training your brain to strengthen the mindsets in the right hand column. So whenever your moment of choice arrives and you see one of the hindering mindsets arise, switch your attention first to the present using one of your senses, then direct your attention to the thoughts associated with the more positive mindset.

Fear of Failure	Take a Chance
FROM getting it right	TO being a continuous learner
FROM not wanting to make a mistake	TO viewing mistakes as growth opportunities
FROM giving up	TO being resilient and bouncing back

Fear of Losing Control	Let It Go
FROM needing to know all the answers	TO letting answers gradually become apparent
FROM how you think things *should* be	TO accepting how things are
FROM believing your way is the best way	TO being curious about other ideas and approaches
FROM believing uncertainty is dangerous	TO recognising that uncertainty holds opportunity

Fear of Standing Out	Find Your Voice
FROM being concerned by what others think	TO believing other people's opinions don't define you
FROM valuing conformity	TO valuing diversity and individuality
FROM it's all about me	TO it's about making a difference

Fear of Missing Out	Think Abundantly
FROM what's best for me	TO what's best for everyone
FROM believing that you need to fight for your piece	TO believing that there is enough to go around
FROM believing that others' successes deplete your opportunities	TO believing that others' successes are evidence that you too can succeed
FROM win/lose	TO win/win

Fear of Facing the Truth	Take Responsibility
FROM seeing others as the source of your problems	**TO** owning your own thoughts, feelings and actions
FROM blaming external factors	**TO** accepting your part in the situation
FROM relying on helplessness to garner support	**TO** taking steps on your own to make things happen
FROM believing you're better than others	**TO** acknowledging your own faults, so you can grow

∨ ∨ ∨ ∨ ∨

› Bill made a significant shift, when he directed his attention away from thinking that if someone won, someone else had to lose. That may have been true in political elections, but in general life he could see many situations where both parties could win. He had been experiencing a difficult relationship with one of the suppliers to his store, after demanding they give him a discount wholesale price. He was driven by wanting to increase his own profit, and gave little thought to the impact a price reduction had on the livelihood of the other person. When a critical delivery was late for the third time, he found himself caught up in the thoughts of how it was damaging him. He spotted this, and then directed his attention to what the supplier might be going through. He chose to change his perspective, and that helped him to see that he'd been unfair. He rectified the situation and, by trying to meet the needs of the supplier, he found that his own needs were met to a much higher standard. Deliveries immediately ceased being late, and he was the first one approached with supplier specials.

∧ ∧ ∧ ∧ ∧

‹ direct attention to antidotes

› Antidotes are interventions that are specifically designed to counteract a particular mindset. They work like a short circuit, halting your habitual mindset in its track and sending your attention down a different pathway. Antidotes are particularly useful when you are struggling more than usual with a mindset, when you see yourself already moving into an emotional state, and when directing your attention to the present is becoming difficult.

Here are examples of antidotes that are popular and effective:

- **Do the opposite** – instead of slipping into the same old response to an issue, do the opposite. For example, instead of arguing with your child over what they want to wear today, act on your moment of choice by doing the opposite and say nothing. Simply doing this one act will interrupt your habitual pattern and put you in a different place. Then direct your attention into the present, and act on your next moment of choice. It does not mean giving in to something; it just means stepping onto a different path and taking a fresh look from there.

- **Get up and move** – when you are struggling with a mindset, it means that it has captured your attention and you don't have full control of that essential tool. Moving your body lifts the flow of oxygen to your brain, and can loosen its attachment to whatever is stealing your attention. You might then find you can refocus your attention back where it belongs: in the present.

- **Positive strategies** – because many of the mindset traps that trip you up are negative default pathways, antidotes that activate and strengthen your positive neural network can help to break these habits. Popular ones include identifying something for which you are grateful today. Another is to balance every negative comment or thought with three positive ones. Also try smiling, even if you are not happy. It will still trigger the brain's positive wiring.

- **Affirmations** – these are positive statements that are designed to insert a positive belief in your mind, which directly counteracts your negative mindset. We suggest below some 'just in time' reminders that might be suitable for each of the five fears. We also suggest some proactive ways to break the grip of these fears.

Fear of Failure	*Just in time reminder*: 'Feel the fear and do it anyway'. *Proactive activity*: Spend a day doing whatever you would do, if you were given an ironclad guarantee you wouldn't fail.
Fear of Losing Control	*Just in time reminder*: 'Let go and embrace what happens'. *Proactive activity*: Designate a stress free day each week, and give up the need to control everything on that day.
Fear of Standing Out	*Just in time reminder*: 'Be authentic'. *Proactive activity*: Do something small every day that is outside your comfort zone.
Fear of Missing Out	*Just in time reminder*: 'We can all win here'. *Proactive activity*: Every week, find a way to serve others with no expectation of reward.
Fear of Facing the Truth	*Just in time reminder*: 'When I own my choices, I own my future'. *Proactive activity*: Designate a criticism-free week. When you feel the urge to complain or whinge, bite your tongue and do something positive.

v   v   v   v   v

› One of the key turning points for Amanda came when she suddenly saw how bitter and negative she had become. Not only was she negative about her ex-husband, but this feeling had transferred into her whole life. She had nothing positive to say about anything or anyone! So she started a gratitude diary, and every night before she went to bed she did two things. Firstly, she wrote down three things that she was grateful for that day. On the first day it was the beautiful weather, her thoughtful mother and the fact that people turned up for meetings on time. They were simple things, but they were things she wouldn't have noticed when her dark moods took hold. Secondly, she would write down three things of which she felt proud. They needed to be things that she had done, that took her one step forward to where she wanted to be. This practice lifted her mood within days, and gave her the space to make some different decisions.

^   ^   ^   ^   ^

› homework to help you prepare for the moment of choice
‹ recognising mindsets you want to change

› Just as you shouldn't walk into the weights room at the gym and just start picking up every weight and using it, identifying the mindsets you really want to change is crucial. Start with the ones that are the easiest to see, and the ones directly affecting the part of your life you are really committed to change. Sometimes it is hard to see what they are. So it might be worth spending some time to reflect on them, diagnose them and understand them a little better.

You don't need to go digging for a mindset to change. Just pick up the ones lying on the surface. Once you start paying attention to your mind, you will know which habits and patterns are ready to change. Going digging for more is like pulling an unripe carrot from the soil. Leave it alone until it's ready to be plucked. If you stick to this strategy, you will find that you are ready to do the work that needs to be done. If at any stage you feel that this is not the case, we recommend you seek the support of a professional counsellor or psychologist.

‹ follow the clues

› Mindsets often lie hidden in full view. You are so familiar with them, you hardly notice they are there. This is why it is so important to wake up, and why we encourage you to build your mindfulness habit, before you start trying to rewire your mind. Once your Observer is switched on and you have the power to switch your attention, you are likely to start noticing your patterns of mind, fears, habits and mindsets.

There are clues and signals that help you identify when mind-sets are hindering or limiting you. Can you relate to any of the following?

- Misinterpreting something that has been said
- Realising after the event, that you have overreacted
- Not being able to see a solution that was clear to others
- Avoiding a situation, when you know it needs attention
- Feeling stuck and not knowing how to get out of it
- Experiencing negative emotions that you can't let go

Whenever you feel like things just aren't working out, and you are not flowing smoothly along in the stream of life, it's time to check if mindsets are at play. Yes, life throws up challenges and hurdles, but how you respond to them is completely in your control. If you experience any sense of struggle or difficulty, it means your mind is struggling. Don't keep battling the situation. Turn instead towards your own mind, because this is where you need to go to find the solution.

Very often just the simple acknowledgement that the struggle is with yourself, and is not the fault of the situation, can be enough to let it go and move on. A simple pause can often release your mind's struggle. But sometimes the mind resists, because it is so attached to a particular habit of mind, fear or thought. So how do you identify the mindset that's throwing a spanner in the works?

‹ work backwards

› Do you find that you can often see what's holding someone else back, but struggle to do the same for yourself? You can listen to a friend and observe their life, seeing very clearly if they are a control freak who needs to let go; or if they are playing the victim, when they need to face the truth and move on. The problem is we sometimes know too much about ourselves. We get caught in our own detailed neural web, rather than standing back and just observing ourselves objectively. With your new skill in mindfulness, this should become a bit easier.

Your fears, mindsets and hindering thoughts manifest themselves as emotions and, ultimately, actions and behaviours.

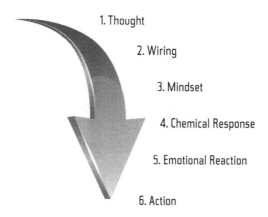

1. Thought

2. Wiring

3. Mindset

4. Chemical Response

5. Emotional Reaction

6. Action

Sometimes the easiest way to start unravelling the mystery of your mindset is to start at the end of this chain and work

backwards. You won't always be able to see the full cycle immediately. Start with the action and behaviour, then observe yourself
for a while and see if you can diagnose the emotion, and then
ultimately, the mindset. Getting it down on paper will make it
much easier to observe objectively, just like watching someone
else. Write anything that comes to mind, even if there seem to
be two conflicting emotions or mindsets. It will become clearer,
the more you observe yourself.

ˇ ˇ ˇ ˇ ˇ

› This example is from Brett and is fairly common in the
business environment, where people feel pressured to always
get things right.

Action/behaviour	Constantly checking what my team are doing and whether they are progressing well.

Brett had no trouble identifying a behaviour that he knew
was too extreme, and that he really wanted to change. Even
though he had been convincing himself that checking in with
his team was a positive behaviour that made him look like he
really cared about them, deep down he knew the behaviour
was driven by something else.

Feelings/emotions	I always feel like something might go wrong. I'm anxious and tense.

When he finally had the opportunity to stop and reflect on
how he felt, when he was checking in on his team, he could
see that he was anxious. But he had never really understood
what he was anxious about, until he understood the five

fears. Then he was able to wake up and clearly observe the activity in his mind.

Thoughts/fears/mindsets	I need to be seen as someone who can be relied on to always get it right. That's always been my reputation, even at home with my family. I'm the dependable one. I fear that I will fail one day and not live up to that expectation.

It was hard for him to admit, but he could now see a pattern throughout his life. It explained why changing careers was so hard, because if it didn't work out he would let his family down. They would lose the trappings of success that he had managed to provide them. But he had reached a point where he was exhausted from trying so hard to hold things together. He just needed to give it a go, and take a chance that it would work out okay.

^ ^ ^ ^ ^

‹ listen to the signals

› Instead of trying to avoid emotions or push them away, see them as signals that help you diagnose your mindsets. They are an indication that your view of the world is in conflict to what is actually happening. It is useful to note the times you are frustrated, angry, nervous or even elated. All emotions give you clues about your interpretation of the world.

When you experience an emotion, ask yourself the following questions:

- Why do I feel like this?
- What am I reacting to?
- What part am I playing to cause this emotion in myself?

Your actions and behaviours also provide an insight into your mindsets. Everyone has something they want to change about themselves. Maybe you stress too much, procrastinate too much, or you simply want to be more successful in an area of your life. Remember, behind every behaviour is a mindset. Use your behaviours to identify your mindsets, by asking the following questions:

- If I could change something about myself that's holding me back, what would it be?
- Why did I make this choice instead of another?
- What do I really believe I will achieve through the actions I am taking now?
- What are some of the thoughts I am having when I do this?

‹ keep a journal

> There is something very powerful about writing things down. The truth is, your head is not the best place to sort something out. When you think through an issue, your brain is selective about which information it throws into the mix. Then it sends the issue through its known pathways, which are often very circular and full of dead ends. It's like using a navigation system that sends you the long way around, when there is a perfectly good highway just one block away.

When you write things down, you take them off the road for a proper inspection. A journal is not an analysis tool, but simply a way to separate yourself from your thoughts. It's like having a conversation with someone who just listens and, as you externalise your thoughts, they start to become clearer and take more shape. You see them from a more objective perspective.

There are various journaling techniques, and it is important that you find the one that best suits your need at any time. Listed below are some of the techniques you could try:

Technique	Benefits / Most Suitable For
Catharsis Writing about the emotions you are feeling *'I feel so frustrated ...'*	• Need for immediate expression of intense emotion • Provides an emotional release
Description Describing and reflecting on events that have happened *'I attempted to resolve the conflict situation with John today'*	• Helps separate you from the experience • Good for reflection • Can help identify fears and mindsets
Free-Intuitive Writing Clearing your mind, then writing whatever comes into your mind without worrying about whether it makes sense. Capture every word or image that appears *'A complex whirlpool of ideas ...'*	• Tapping into creativity • Bringing clarity to thoughts you do not yet understand
Reflection Writing about insights, by looking back on your life or specific experiences *'The way I acted in this situation made me think ...'*	• Strengthening your Observer and deepening your awareness • Bringing order to your experiences • Identifying mindsets

‹ get an objective view

› Just as keeping a journal is a way to externalise your thoughts, so you can see them more objectively, talking to someone can also be useful. But it is important to choose someone who is willing to play the role that you need. They must be a mindful listener, and be prepared to offer no opinion about the issue. They should be a skilled questioner, who uses these questions as gentle prompts at the right time, to help you explore the issue further. Their role is to help you bring order to your thoughts, by enabling you to externalise them in a safe space. Your insights come not from this person but from yourself, as you hear your own words in a way that you can't hear them when they remain in your head.

As you can probably tell from this description, most family members and friends will not fall into this category, because they find it too hard to resist offering an opinion. The last thing you need is to be told what to do, how to fix it, that you're right and someone else is wrong, or to 'get a grip'! If you don't know a trusted adviser who can take on this role, you may find value in engaging a coach, a counsellor or a psychologist.

› it takes time

Although your brain remains plastic throughout your whole life, changing your wiring requires discipline, some effort and a lot of patience. Creating new pathways can feel like hard work, but the work gets easier. You will probably find that many of your patterns of mind won't just disappear. In fact, they may be around forever. But what does change is your attachment to them. The goal of thinking differently is to create new pathways, to give yourself more choice about how you think and act in a situation. Like disused railway tracks, old mindsets may still exist on the map; you just don't choose to travel down them anymore.

You are laying new tracks through the wilderness. It takes some time to map out the route, clear the path, lay the road, and encourage the drivers to make this their preferred way home.

Your brain will not rewire after just one try, just as your biceps muscle will not develop after one bicep curl. But repetition over time does deliver real change. And thinking differently can become a healthy habit, that makes you the architect of your mind and the owner of your destiny.

> grow

> When you wake up and think differently, you don't just rewire your mind to create the life you want. You also start a new habit in your life that is incredibly beneficial. Keeping your neurons moving, growing and changing is a habit that will bring a sparkle to your eyes and a lightness to your step.

Not only will new knowledge and skills support your efforts to get wired for life, they are essential for remaining open to even more new and exciting ways of seeing the world. Without fresh material to stimulate it, your mind will just move back into rigid patterns. It seems a shame to do all that good work of waking up and thinking differently, and then just fall back into another pattern.

Make a commitment to a healthy mind and get wired for life, by incorporating these exercises into your day, your week and the rest of your years.

› grow in ways that support your new mindsets

∨ ∨ ∨ ∨ ∨

› Jodie came to a crossroad on her journey to release control. She inherently knew that it was the right thing to do, and understood that letting go was a wise step to take. Yet her brain still protested: 'But successful people have goals, plans and performance indicators, and that's why they are successful!' It tried to draw her back into her old habits, by throwing up all the examples of people who did these things and seemed successful. So she went looking for examples to challenge it. She watched other people and read biographies, and this all helped to cultivate her growing new mindset. Stories of people who did it differently gave the growing mindset more substance and evidence to remain strong. This final step was then reinforced, as she gained evidence from her own experiences. Each time she redirected her efforts to the things she really could control, and stopped fighting the things she could not, her skills were strengthened and her mind grew. Doing this without first waking up and thinking differently would have been pointless. But the three steps together changed her life.

∧ ∧ ∧ ∧ ∧

When you have decided to let go of an old mindset and adopt an alternative, new knowledge and skills are crucial tools for building your confidence and competence. They help to promote the growth of the new mindset, and encourage it to become the preferred pathway in your mind. New knowledge and skills can stimulate the neural pathways, transforming a new mindset from a sapling to a flourishing tree. This helps you resist the temptation to slip back into the old patterns.

› exercises that grow your mind to support new mindsets

Every person will have need of different knowledge and skills, to build and strengthen their mind. Rather than proposing specific exercises, we encourage you to ask yourself some questions, that will help you identify the right ones to add to your life.

* In which parts of my life do I feel least confident or competent? What knowledge or skills would address this gap?
* If I am to begin down this new path, what knowledge and skills will help me stick to it?
* Where have I faltered in the past, and what is a new skill or piece of knowledge that will help me do it differently next time?

ˇ ˇ ˇ ˇ ˇ

› Amanda was progressing well with exercising her ability to wake up and think differently. She was at the point where she could diffuse her destructive emotions, recognise her limiting mindsets and release their hold on her. Then she realised that a key part of her victim mentality came from allowing herself to be such a dependent person. She had expected others to do everything for her, and didn't even know how to manage her finances. This caused her significant anxiety now that she was on her own, and the arrival of bills was one of the triggers that set her off down the 'poor me' path. So she undertook a personal budgeting course, and really felt her confidence grow. Now she could take full responsibility for this area of her life and she even enjoyed it!

^ ^ ^ ^ ^

Fears, mindsets and habitual patterns can all be shifted; by waking up and thinking differently. But once you take those steps, you may also see the need to explore new knowledge and new skills, if you want the new mindset to really thrive. We've suggested some ideas that can help you to grow healthy new mindsets, to replace each of the five fears.

Take a Chance	This mindset is hindered by the fear of failure. To help you burst through and take the risks that will create the life you want, new knowledge and skills might be just the thing to boost your confidence. It might be how to start a new business, techniques for parenting, skills to improve a sport or hobby, or skills to better manage relationships. There's a book, course or online program on just about every topic, and there are people who already display those skills all around you.
Let It Go	This mindset is hindered by the fear of losing control. Once you have conquered the tendency for your own mind to paint its elaborate picture and push you down this path, it's time to open yourself to alternatives. There are many pathways up the same mountain, and they can all be right in their own way. Consider a book or course on different personality styles, attend seminars that address issues in a completely different way to your normal style, and ask people about their approach. And wherever possible, seek facts before you let your mind fill the unknown with its own limited options.
Find Your Voice	This mindset is hindered by the fear of standing out and the need to belong. Efforts to wake up and think differently will be supported by new knowledge and skills that boost your confidence. Consider a public speaking course, ask a friend to explain how the world of marketing and PR works, or learn techniques for courageous conversations and saying what you really think.

Think Abundantly	This mindset is hindered by the fear of missing out. Skills in networking, relationship building, and connecting will help you experience the power of collaboration and sharing. Participate in a charity event and give your time and energy without any expectation of return. Expand your knowledge into areas that reveal the truth about how interconnected we are. The science of living systems and many philosophies will open your mind.
Take Responsibility	This mindset is hindered by the fear of facing the truth. The trick here is to embrace the things you have been pushing away. If 'It's not your fault' that you're always late or loosing things, learn some time management techniques or engage a clutter expert. If 'It's not your fault' that you're always struggling to make ends meet, learn how to budget. If 'I already know that', then embrace a beginner's attitude and look for at least one thing you can learn. If your relationships never last, learn some new communication techniques.

˅ ˅ ˅ ˅ ˅

> Additional knowledge and skills helped Brett who had previously let the fear of failure stand in the way of starting a business that he was passionate about. He recognised that he knew nothing about small business, and his fear of failure was being compounded by the fear of losing control. He took the first step of finding out the nuts and bolts of running a business, by enrolling a business coach who took the mystique out of it all. The fear was instantly reduced and the mindset could further loosen its grasp.

Reading a book on mindful parenting was a key part of the *Mind Gardener Method* for Jodie, the self–confessed control freak mum.

Bill went on an overseas trip and observed an interesting business model being used by a local community. He saw that people could work together and share in the profit. This gave him more ideas about how to turn his beachside corner shop, and the whole area, into an even bigger success.

^ ^ ^ ^ ^

› the power of purpose

Parents of a teenage girl recently sought my advice. They were almost tearing their hair out. Their major parenting goal was for their daughter to get a university degree. She had decided a year ago that this wasn't a path she wanted to follow. For the past 12 months, they had been plotting and trying hard to influence her to move in the direction they believed was best. The fact that she wasn't going to do as they wished had left them miserable. They believed they had failed as parents. I asked them what they might do differently if they focused on the purpose of parenting rather than a specific goal. I asked them to consider the question 'What legacy did they really want to leave their daughter?'

For me, it's to ensure my kids have all the tools to lead a happy and healthy life. This statement provides me guidance in all parenting decisions. When I reach a roadblock (like your daughter refusing something you believe is good for her) it helps me to adapt and find another solution. It also provides a balanced perspective when evaluating myself as a parent and allows me to focus on something I can control. I can ask myself how well I went in my purpose each day 'Did I do the best I could to provide tools to help my daughter lead a happy and healthy life?'

One of the exercises that will support your efforts, as you grow new healthy mindsets that wire you for life, is to uncover and live by your purpose. Living with purpose provides you a clear focus, to help you navigate through the shifting sands of life. While whole books are dedicated to this one concept, you can get started with your focus on purpose by considering these questions:

- When do I feel I am making a real difference?
- What am I drawn to do, because of the effect it has on others?
- If I was to be praised for making a difference, what is the thing I'd most like to hear someone tell me?
- If tomorrow I had more than enough money to retire, what would I continue to do in the world?
- What legacy do I hope to leave in the world?
- What do I hope people say about me at my own funeral?

Operating with purpose in mind has been identified as one of the success factors in business. Your *purpose* is 'why you exist', whereas your *vision* is 'where you want to be'. Desired destinations can change, but purpose is enduring. This is why it is such a powerful way to anchor yourself and refocus your mind.

If you're not sure what your purpose is, seek some resources to help you uncover it. The moment you bring to mind your purpose, your focus expands and it has the effect of repositioning your perspective on many things. It can help you move through uncertainty, get your priorities right, and redirect your efforts to where they will make a difference.

› grow in ways that open your mind

Sometimes new knowledge and skills provide you with the wake up call you need. How often have you sat through a documentary, fascinated by facts you had never realised: natural phenomena, cultural differences, stories behind company collapses, changes in the earth's cycles. Sometimes it's enough to open your mind and change your view of the world. Many people have found a cause for life by hearing a story that fed them knowledge they had not previously possessed.

Have you noticed that people who enjoy their life are often open and curious about many things? They show genuine interest when others talk about their passions; they will tell you about a fascinating little fact they heard recently; and they sometimes surprise you with the things they read, watch and attend. You often find yourself wondering 'How do you know so much about everything?' and 'How do you find the time to explore all of these seemingly disconnected things?'

The most creative thinkers and inventors often use the merging of two completely unrelated subject matters to inspire a new idea. In fact, being too much of an expert can sometimes hinder this ability to create, adapt and grow. Stimulating your mind with new knowledge, learning new skills, and exposing yourself to new ideas and different perspectives will keep your neurons firing, and your life fresh and interesting.

‹ exercises that open your mind and keep it fresh

› There is no limit to where, when and how you can stimulate your mind. Diversity and novelty are key. As you open your mind, you will find yourself drawn to particular areas. So explore the things that naturally fascinate you, and don't feel there are things you 'should' do. But maintain a healthy balance between diving deep and roaming broadly. If you go too deep, sometimes you leave no room for diversity, which results in not really stimulating the brain in new ways. And if you roam too broadly, you just skim the tops of the waves and won't stimulate enough neuron growth to retain anything particularly useful.

The exercises suggested here demand a 'beginner's mind'. This means approaching all of them like an inquisitive child on their very first visit to a toy store: big eyes that miss nothing, excited smile and positive exclamations. Children learn so much more than adults, because every sense is open and their curiosity is their guide.

› new information

Do you watch the same TV programs each week, read the same type of books, and go to the same old places? We all have preferences, but try this:

- Every month, buy or borrow a magazine on a topic you know very little about, and read it from front to back.
- Every three months, grab a friend and attend a lecture or seminar on something neither of you have ever explored.
- Once each week, disrupt your TV watching habits by switching off one of your favourite regular shows and using this time to read a book.

› new experiences

Do you always travel the same route to work, the shops, a friend's house, and other regular destinations? Do you spend your free time doing the same old thing at the same old locations? We all have habits, but try this:

- Every week, change at least one of the routes that you travel regularly, even if it's just going left around the corner to your local shop instead of right.
- Every month, visit a different venue or public space in your city.
- Every three months, attend an event you have not tried before: soccer, basketball, a market, opera, ballet, rock concert, jazz, a comedy show. It can even be something simple at the local sports field or local hall.

› new challenges

Do you stick with the things you know you are good at? Do you avoid the things that seem a bit difficult using the excuse 'That's just not my thing'? We all have particular areas of expertise but try this:

- Take up a new hobby.
- Learn a new language.
- Learn a musical instrument.
- Cook something you have never tried before.
- Write a book, even if it's just a little fun story for your kids to read.
- Take on a challenge for charity, then get together with friends to make it happen.

Of course, it will feel uncomfortable when you present something new to your brain. That's because your brain will be searching for an existing neural network, into which the information can be neatly slotted. On failing to find anything that corresponds to the new information, it will take energy to form new networks. But once these are established, your new task will become easier and easier.

We hope that these ideas provide you with enough inspiration to identify something you can try. Remember it's about stimulating your brain, not about becoming an expert. Just be curious and allow your brain to flourish, as it is showered with the kaleidoscope of experiences that colour your world.

› grow in ways that maintain basic brain functions

When my grandmother passed away, I went to her house and sat for what seemed like hours in her favourite armchair. After reliving our many conversations and remembering so many lovely interactions, my attention turned to the small table beside her chair. There sat a notebook full of her handwriting and dog-eared newspaper clippings. As I flicked through, I saw evidence of a range of habits Nana had incorporated into her day right up until her passing in her 88th year.

Firstly, there were random words written over all the pages, words that were unfamiliar to me and obviously to her too.

She had started a habit of writing down new words when she heard them, then looking them up in the dictionary next to her notebook. Now I understood how a woman, who had migrated from a non-English speaking country when she was 34, had a better command of the English language than many born here.

Secondly, there were recipes. Some she had seen on TV cooking shows, others heard on the radio, and some borrowed from friends. Despite the favourite family recipes she had mastered over 70 years, she never failed to produce a new dish with the latest 'in fashion' ingredient whenever we visited. While most grandkids were enjoying their grandmother's roast chicken, I was never surprised when she produced the latest dish from a celebrity chef.

Thirdly, there were clippings of crosswords, puzzles and other word games. Some from the newspaper and others probably secretly ripped from the magazine pile in her doctor's waiting room! She did a puzzle or crossword every day. This was preceded by a walk to the end of her street and back, and regular stretches to loosen up muscles and joints.

The daily habits revealed in her notebook were a strong indication that she understood the importance of keeping her mind stimulated and active. And her daily mind training (although she would never have called it that) was apparent to anyone who knew her. She was as sharp as a tack, knew something about everything, and didn't suffer the forgetfulness afflicting many of her peers.

› the ignored organ

How often have you considered the amazing things your brain does? This morning I was grateful that my brain remembered that today was the day my daughter needed to wear her sports uniform to school. I was happy my brain was attentive and noticed the smoke coming from the motor of my treadmill, allowing me to abandon my exercise routine before it became unsafe. I was pleased my brain's language centres could interpret the jumbled words coming from my toddler's mouth. During my drive to work, I was lucky my brain had the capacity to understand the signs indicating the road ahead was blocked, and to remember an alternative route that could get me to my destination. And on arriving at the office and receiving a phone call from a client with a looming problem, my brain proposed a solution that addressed their needs. And all this before 9am!

You rely on these, and many other critical functions of your brain, every moment in every day. But like every other part of your body, your brain's performance can diminish, if it is not well cared for and maintained.

› exercises to maintain basic brain functions and brain health

You can go out and spend thousands on the latest brain-training gizmo, or you can use the thousands of opportunities in your day to stimulate your mind and keep it healthy. Here we propose just a few ideas, that can help you maintain the basic functions of your brain and support your brain's health.

‹ memory

› Memory is one of the more well-recognised functions of the brain. You constantly rely on your brain to recall important facts and store information for the future. You can boost your memory, by trying some of the following exercises:

- Once each week, pick a new song you like and memorise the lyrics.
- Instead of relying on your phone to store everyone's numbers, commit yourself to memorising three each week, just like the old days!

- Every time you attend a gathering, challenge yourself to remember the name of every person you meet.
- Play memory games with yourself: 'when was the first time I visited this place?' 'what was I wearing this time last week?' 'which page number is my favourite recipe in this book?' 'how many glasses of water did I drink today?'

The more you exercise your memory muscle, the more it improves, so look for as many opportunities as possible.

‹ attention

› In Chapter 8, we explored the importance of attention. To survive in the world, it is important to be able to pay attention to what is going on around you. Your mindfulness practice is a perfect way to exercise this capability. But also add these exercises:

- It is easier to pay attention when your body is alert; so turn the old school teacher rebuke 'Sit up straight and pay attention!' into your mantra.
- Whenever you are moving from place to place, whether on foot, driving, on public transport or riding a bike, bring to mind the caution 'Watch out!' and do just that. Whenever your attention is directed to watching out, it is switched on.
- Turn off the mobile phone or leave it behind, when you go out for a pleasant social event. Technology is becoming one of the biggest threats to well-honed attention. So don't let it rule your life.

‹ language

› Communicating with others is a critical activity and takes up a large portion of your life. But in your interactions with family, friends, colleagues and the general community, you often find yourself using the same old lines and having the same old conversations. Expand your vocabulary and mix up your conversations, using the following exercises:

- Each week, identify a new word, find out its meaning, then use it in conversation. You can find new words in the newspaper, by keeping your ears open, or just flicking through the dictionary.
- Each week, read a poem out loud. Allow the rhythm, as well as the words, to flow over you.
- Listen to the sound of your own voice, when you are in conversation with the people you interact with every day. Hearing yourself makes your language centres more alert and often triggers a different pace, different tone and different words.

‹ spatial reasoning

› Do you have a good sense of direction? Some people are born with it and some people aren't. Spatial awareness is all about being able to operate in the three-dimensional world. If you can't estimate the right-sized bowl for your leftovers, can't judge whether a parking gap will fit your car, or realise too late that the couch you just bought won't fit up the stairs, a bit of spatial practice might help. Try this:

- Start orienteering. Getting lost in the countryside, and having to find your way out, will force your brain to deal with this challenge. But take a course first!
- Play video games. You might think they are just for young people, but a fun day out at the arcade might be just what your brain needs, to test itself with three-dimensional challenges.
- Play blocks with your children, building 3D shapes and testing the limit of what you can make.
- Look at a map before you travel a route, and again at the end.

‹ problem-solving

› Every day you are faced with challenges, some small and some big. You often use your problem-solving skills without realising it. But it is always useful to include some intentional exercise of this function, to make sure your problem-solving skills are at their peak. Try this:

- Talk a friend through a problem they are experiencing. Play the role only of asking questions, and let them respond and find the solution. Watching someone else go through the process of problem-solving embeds the steps in your own mind.
- Next time you have a problem to solve, write down everything you think and the steps you will take. It helps you to check that you are covering all the important issues and following an effective process.

‹ positive emotions

› One of the growing areas of health concern in the modern world is stress, anxiety and depression. Negative emotions are on the rise, and seem to be getting the better of many people. But what some don't realise is that negativity is a trained habit. There are many reasons why you should cultivate positive emotions, and it's not just to feel good. Positive people are more active, more resilient and more creative. If this is an area where you could do with a boost, try this:

- Keep a gratitude diary, writing down at least one thing each day for which you are grateful. There are many web sites and resources to help with this exercise.
- Whenever you catch yourself thinking a negative thought, counter it with three positive ones. This trains your brain to look for positive thoughts too.

- Smile and laugh more. See if you can double the number of times you laugh and smile in a day.
- Play uplifting music, put flowers in your home, visit an art gallery and shower your brain with beauty in all its forms. Harmony and beauty are soothing for your brain.
- Read books with a positive message, watch uplifting movies, read inspiring biographies, and limit your intake of sad, tense and scary stories.
- Hang out with happy people. Happiness is a virus, so expose yourself!

‹ exercise

› A combination of aerobic and strength exercises are known to boost brain health and performance. There are too many studies to mention on the benefits of walking, running, playing a sport, lifting weights and just raising your physical movement up a notch from where you are now. It is linked to new neuron growth, improved memory, enhanced reasoning and cognitive performance, and reduced risk of some brain diseases. Increased blood circulation sends more oxygen and glucose into the brain, and removes waste more quickly. Various chemicals released by the brain during exercise have positive effects on your skills and on your mood. Clear your mind by increasing your physical movement every day.

‹ food and drink

› The brain requires a disproportionate amount of energy for its size. It weighs only 2 per cent of your body but monopolises 20 per cent of your energy intake. And it can't function for long before needing another boost. Studies reveal that the quality of your decisions will decline as glucose levels decline. So it's important to work out how regularly your metabolism needs a boost. In general, the best diet for your body is also the best diet for your brain.

When you feel that slump during the day, do you reach for a coffee or a soft drink? While these drinks do have the immediate effect of increasing alertness, it is short-lived and will be followed by a more significant performance decline not long after. By far the most important fluid for your brain is water. Staying hydrated is crucial for brain performance and health.

And last but not least, alcohol! The effects of alcohol on the brain are obvious, as you move from one glass to many. Initial relaxation moves to slow reaction times, blurred vision and impaired memory. The effects of an occasional session may be reversible, but heavy drinking can have far-reaching effects on the brain. Apart from the potential damage to existing neurons, a few drinks can disrupt the growth of new neurons, hindering all your effort to keep your brain fresh and flourishing.

Just as a garden requires regular fertilising, so too does your mind. If you want your mind garden to thrive, think about its inputs, and ensure it is getting the nourishment that such an important organ deserves. Your life will benefit from it! And when you are practising the three steps of the *Mind Gardener Method* together, you will find that your obstacles fade and that you are wired for the life you want.

> thriving not just surviving

'It's like I'm now playing by a totally different set of rules, and they are the flipside of all of the rules that I had previously thought were the right way to live. But I have no doubt in my mind that the new rules are the right rules. They make everything flow so much more easily. My decisions are no longer based on fear. They are based on what is right and what really makes a difference in my life. I no longer judge myself by what other people think; in fact it doesn't even enter the equation. That's not to say that I feel comfortable all of the time. In fact I see it as a sign that if I'm not out of my comfort zone, I am not really living. I am achieving more than I ever have before in my life, but I feel like I'm doing less. I am attracting opportunities by having faith. Everything in my life has moved to a higher level. And there is only one thing I changed. My mind.' Brett

> finding success

It was six months since we had all met at the high school reunion, and Brett was sharing his experiences over a bite of lunch with what had become a tight-knit group. As he sat there talking, he was almost unrecognisable from the man I remember. He finally took the leap and followed his passion, starting his own business and finding that his ideas really did have currency. He was making a huge difference in the lives of young people and, rather than threatening the lifestyle he had created for his family, everything was just fine. He was earning the same if not more money, and it was all on his own terms. Now he no longer seemed to be 'trying' to get somewhere but, strangely enough, it was all happening for him.

His old corporate colleagues give him a hard time, for taking what they call the easy road, and it can bring him down a bit that they might think he had failed in some way. But he also had one of them take him out for coffee and ask him how he'd had the guts to do it. This mate admitted that they were all a touch jealous, and Brett's actions had motivated a few of them to take stock.

Most importantly, Brett is happy. His whole face has changed, and his previous quizzical look has been replaced with a wide grin. People notice that he never stops smiling and that his wife and children now take top priority. He has made a significant shift in his whole life, which is not to say the fear of failure doesn't arise from time to time. It was only one week ago, that someone approached him about submitting a proposal to roll out his programs nationally. He saw himself start to make excuses, but quickly realised that the fear was doing the talking, and he was able to halt that in its tracks.

› finding freedom

Jodie looked like a weight had been lifted from her shoulders. Someone asked if she'd just got back from a holiday but 'no', she said, she just felt like she was free from the burdens of everyday life for once. For the first time in her life, she felt that her work and family life were now in balance. Learning how to let go of controlling every last detail at work had freed her up to focus on the right things. She had been given feedback that her staff were much happier with her leadership, and she didn't feel the need to take work home or be glued to her iPhone all weekend.

For the first time, she felt alive. A month ago, she and her husband had taken a romantic weekend away, leaving the baby with her mother-in-law. While she had struggled with the urge to ring and check in every hour, she was conscious that this was just her control freak talking, and that there was no reason to create big dramas in her head. They sat down for a long meal together and laughed without a care in the world.

When she was with her baby, she was really there. It was easier to get everything done now, than when she was always driven by the schedule. She was actually enjoying motherhood for the first time. And it was good timing, because she had just discovered she was pregnant with her second child. Soon her resolve would really be tested!

› finding authenticity

In the past, Sarah would have waited for everyone else to speak first. But now she piped up, keen to tell her story. She had clearly found her voice and exuded a new confidence. As a result of the success in her art sales, she had found the courage to ask her manager if she could work part-time, so she could dedicate more energy to making her dream a reality. This enabled her to take on other projects, including lecturing at a local art school.

We all laughed at how far things had come; that someone so fearful of standing out was now lecturing in front of groups. She attributes her change to continually embracing opportunities that took her out of her comfort zone. Now it just seems like second nature.

Sarah had finally realised that one of the reasons she had been so reserved around people was that she really hadn't known herself very well. 'That's why I had found it so hard to speak up or stand out, because I didn't know what I really believed or what I was trying to say. I was always afraid people would see through that. But after telling my story a few times, I've become so much clearer about where I'm heading, and it's made me more passionate. I don't care too much about what people think of all that anymore. I am who I am and I'm happy with that.'

We all gave Sarah a big round of applause, something she was becoming accustomed to hearing!

› finding fulfilment

Bill's mind had finally joined his body on the sea change. Instead of constantly being on watch for who was out to get him and what he might be missing out on, he was finally relaxed about things and felt confident that everything was okay.

When he'd learnt to stop only thinking of himself, he'd noticed many opportunities to help others. His original reason for entering politics, a desire to serve others, had been reignited. He really felt like he was finally making a difference. He was coaching the local soccer team (offering more wisdom than skills, if the truth be known!) and he had started a mentoring service for local business owners. 'I really feel proud of my community and by joining forces we've done some amazing things. It's fulfilling to be doing something more than just a job. I've learnt a lot from the people there and I feel like I'm giving something back too. It took me a while to see that it was me who was creating the friction. They always had this wonderful abundance mentality.'

› finding happiness

Amanda actually started her story by apologising to the group. We were all surprised, but she said 'I have been very difficult to be around, and none of you have ever judged me. I look back on this last six months as the most important in my life, and much of my progress came from listening to you all, and how open you were about your fears. It made me realise I had shut myself down, and that I really did need to take responsibility for my life. So thank you.'

Amanda explained how she had taken her sister on her journey too, and that she was really pleased to see her sister smiling a lot more. She had found that helping someone else had also made it easier to keep herself on track when things got hard.

Amanda's face had softened, and we had rarely heard her talk about her divorce over the last month. In fact, the topic she spent most time on was her desire to find another relationship. Then she said something that really demonstrated her shift. 'The truth is that I need to do a lot more work on myself before I can possibly be a good partner. Instead of relying on people to make me happy, I need to find that happiness and inner peace myself.' I don't think I was the only one who felt that Amanda was well on her way to finding it.

› the never-ending story

As our lunch came to a close, it was clear that this would not be the end of our journey together. We all recognised that it's too easy to slip back into old habits and no-one wanted that to happen now. We needed each other for support and encouragement, or even just a gentle reminder from time to time. Each one of them had already learnt the hard way that there was no magic pill. Commitment and discipline would be needed, if they were going to achieve the life well lived.

› the magic pill

It's an oft-quoted fact that self-help is a billion dollar industry. People all over the world spend billions of dollars each year, in an attempt to overcome their challenges and create the life of their dreams. Have you ever stopped to wonder why it's such a thriving industry? Yes, people are seeking to improve themselves, but there's something else going on. People are looking for the silver bullet, the magic pill, or that quick fix. Sadly, there isn't one.

Brett found that reading a book didn't change his life. Reading another one that promised more didn't either. And reading yet another one that someone had raved about didn't help at all. There is no escaping reality: you need to do the work. Would you read a weight loss book and expect to have dropped five kilograms as you close the last page? Could you finish a book on woodwork and expect to complete a beautifully crafted table the moment you finish? No and no. No book will create immediate change. But your own daily choices and actions will.

I recently embarked on a new health and fitness regime. To get results, it required hard work. I had to commit to exercising every single day. I had to push myself when the going got tough. Some weeks I had to bounce back from disappointment, when I didn't get the results I was seeking. The truth was I had to recommit to what I was doing, in every moment, and with every choice I made. Training your mind is exactly the same. Not choosing to cultivate your mind means you have actually made a choice. You are encouraging your brain to stick to its well-worn paths and agreeing to accept all that comes from travelling there again.

Success, fulfilment, authenticity, freedom and happiness are not achieved overnight. Brains take time to rewire, just as plants take time to grow. Those who experience the most profound effects commit to the *Mind Gardener Method* for a lifetime.

› making the shift

Throughout this book, we have shared the stories of many people. Some remain tied to their habits, ignorant that their mind has laid traps in their path. Some have woken up for a moment, but retreated in the face of the truth, too afraid or too lazy to take the next step. When the timing is right for them, we know they will venture forth. Others have given the *Mind Gardener Method* a go, but struggle when they hit a snag. They expect miracles, but are not committed to the regular practice that is essential for real and lasting change. And finally, a large proportion have adopted the *Mind Gardener Method* as a normal part of their life, and recognise that they could not survive and thrive without it.

Many of the concepts in this book contradict what we've been told all our lives by our parents, teachers, bosses, the system, our culture and our friends. It took Brett, Jodie, Sarah, Bill and Amanda many months to start rewriting their lives, by rewiring their minds. The traditional ways of viewing life might be strongly wired in you, but just considering the alternative can help you make the shift.

The table below reveals the sorts of indicators that can help you recognise whether you are trapped by traditional mindsets, or if you are becoming wired for life. What you think, feel, do and say reveals much about what drives you, so check in regularly and make sure you're heading in the right direction to create the life you want.

	Traditional Life	Wired For Life
Think	I must work hard to get ahead You only live once. I want to be successful You can't have it all	I must work hard to stay present You only live once. I want to make a difference I create my own reality
Feel	Stressed Fearful Frustrated Trapped Numb	Relaxed Confident Happy Free Inspired

	Traditional Life	Wired For Life
Do	Busy-ness	Effortlessness
	Reactive	Proactive
	The importance of doing	The importance of being
	Delaying happiness	Being happy right now
	What I *should* do	What feels right
	Focus on risk	Focus on opportunity
Say	It wasn't meant to be easy	Stop trying so hard
	If only that hadn't happened	No excuses
	I'll just wait and see	It's up to me
	I doubt it	That's interesting

Finishing this book is just the start of your journey. Maybe you have woken up to a new way of living, and are eager to get wired for life. The road won't always be easy, and many traps and obstacles lie ahead. But you are not alone.

We've provided an Appendix, addressing the common traps and how to get through them. We've also included a seven-day mind work out to get you started. You can add your own exercises, or repeat these over and over until you get some momentum.

Join our programs at www.mindgardener.com to keep it fresh, expand your exercises and join with others who are on the same path. As Brett, Jodie, Sarah, Bill and Amanda found, this support network becomes a precious resource over time.

Above all, step up and take responsibility for your mind and your life. Because you **are** a mind gardener. You can cultivate your own life well lived, whatever that may be for you. We have shown you how to plant the seeds, prune and weed, and cultivate the soil for a healthy and happy mind garden. You now have the tools you need to make it thrive. How your mind garden grows is now up to you.

Happy cultivating!

› seven-day mind work-out

› This work-out program is designed to provide you with the three types of mind training exercises in the proportion of:

50 per cent Wake Up
40 per cent Think Differently
10 per cent Grow

Start doing each exercise on the nominated day, and then continue it for the rest of the week. In some cases there are options, depending on which fear you want to conquer. After your first seven days, continue with the exercises that have fitted nicely into your week and start making up your own.

Visit www.mindgardener.com for more ideas.

› day 1
‹ tame the busy mind (wake up exercise)

Many of the 50,000 thoughts and 12,000 internal conversations you have every day, reinforce the things that hold you back. Rather than trying to push the thoughts away, simply spot them, focus back on what you are doing, and let the chatter subside. Continually ask yourself 'Where is my mind right now?' If it's not present with what you are doing, use one of your five senses to bring it into focus.

› day 2
‹ choose a relevant 'ban' exercise from the list below (think differently exercises)
‹ fear of failure - ban the excuse

› Notice when you are about to use an excuse, to avoid doing something uncomfortable. Instead, just jump in and give it a go. Accept every scary invitation, agree to every challenging project or task, and try anything you would normally avoid.

‹ fear of losing control - ban the plan

› Notice when you strike something that does not go according to your plan. Rather than trying to steer the situation back in line with the plan, go with the events unfolding in front of you. Practise responding to them with a clear mind; not through the filter of your plan.

‹ fear of standing out - ban the blend

› Notice all the times you are tempted to blend in with the crowd. Maybe you're avoiding sitting in the front row, or disagreeing with common opinion. Instead, do the opposite. See what it feels like to go against the grain.

‹ fear of missing out - ban the me focus

› Take yourself out of the equation and focus instead on giving to others. You might volunteer for a cause, help someone out with a problem before getting on with your own work, leave the last piece of cake for someone else, or give a compliment without expectation of reward.

‹ fear of facing the truth - ban the whinge

› Excessive complaining draws attention to the pain you are experiencing and sharpens its intensity. Every time you spot yourself whingeing or complaining, either to yourself or to others, stop mid-sentence and instead find at least one good thing to say.

› day 3
‹ mind check (wake up exercise)

› When you get out of bed in the morning and before you go to bed at night, sit comfortably, close your eyes and notice your breath moving in and out of your body for one minute. Every time your mind wanders, simply return it to your breath.

› day 4
‹ mirror, mirror (grow exercise)

› Identify someone who doesn't have the fear or mindset you are struggling to conquer. They may be famous, or they may be someone you know. Do a bit of research on them or ask them some questions to better understand their mindset. Then put yourself in their shoes for the week, by asking yourself 'How would that person respond in this situation?'

› day 5
‹ excellence challenge (wake up exercise)

› Strengthen your ability to focus on one thing at a time, by striving for excellence. Undertake each daily task, as if you will be tested on it at the end of the day. This will keep you focused, and motivate you to finish the task properly, before moving on to something else.

› day 6
‹ triple happiness (think differently exercise)
› Whenever you catch yourself thinking or saying something negative, counter it by immediately thinking or saying at least three positive things about the same situation.

› day 7
‹ slice of nature (wake up exercise)
› You will tend to feel calmer, clearer and more relaxed when in nature. Aim for 20 minutes in nature each day. A series of short mental breaks outdoors, a walk from home to the bus, or ducking out for lunch will quickly add up to 20 minutes. But it only counts if you clear your mind and fully notice the sights, sounds and smells on your path.

› set yourself up for success
To give yourself the best possible chance at changing your mind and your life, we recommend the following tips:

1. Start the day with a mind exercise. Then spend at least one minute committing to the exercise you will do that day. Don't fall into the trap of thinking 'I'll try the pause when I need to.' Turn that into a tangible commitment: 'I will pause every time before I get a glass of water today.'
2. Start a journal. Jot down the things that trip you up during the day. Jot down your success stories. Use it to reflect, reinforce and recommit.
3. Buddy up. Ask a friend to do the same exercises each day, or get your whole household working on a mind exercise regime together. Discuss what you are going to do at the breakfast table, and review it at the dinner table that night. If you have kids, what a great way to role model the importance of their

mind as their greatest asset. In some organisations, whole teams try the same exercises and discuss the impact at a short weekly meeting. And they are still sticking with it years later and achieving great results.

4. Draw upon resources. There are many resources available to support your practice, some of which are outlined in the resources section of this book.

5. Keep it fresh. Even a mind exercise you really like, has the potential to become stale, if you become complacent. Every month, challenge yourself to try a completely new and different exercise, and see how much this stimulates your mind.

> traps that lie in wait

> There are some common traps you might experience, when you start actively cultivating your mind. It's easy to slip into them, and you wouldn't be alone if they catch you out. But forewarned is forearmed. So keep a watchful eye and don't get disillusioned if they creep up on you at some stage. This Appendix is a quick reference to help you get back on track when you feel like something's not quite right!

> only training your mind in the hard times

It's natural to get committed to your mind training efforts, when you face a particular challenge. But if you then let it all go in the good times, you can't expect your mind to bounce back when the next challenge hits. The point of creating a healthy routine in your life is to keep it going all the time.

One of our clients was known for her regular meltdowns. She would crumple in a heap over the stress of her job, or the latest relationship breakdown, or a family drama. Every time she emerged from the episode she would start using her meditation CD, knowing full well that it was the key to getting her mind back on track. She would practise every day ... for a week. By then she would be feeling great, until a few weeks later when it all happened again. It never occurred to her to make her meditation an ongoing practice, because she had a mindset that mental exercise was only something you did to help you out of a hole.

Once she saw the flaw in this thinking, she turned a corner. Meditating regularly, she could see when things started to build up, and she was able to act differently at a much earlier stage. Before too long, the meltdowns disappeared. She no longer attracted the stress, family dramas, and emotionally unavailable men. Until this day, she maintains her mind training discipline and is a truly fulfilled person.

› discipline is the key

Practice makes perfect. Training anything to an expert standard takes 10,000 hours of practice. If you want to be the expert of your own mind (which is the best thing you could possibly do!) then it is going to take commitment and discipline. You may not think it's important to be mindful for every activity (eg. doing the dishes). But every time you let the mind wander by itself, you train your mind that it's okay to do that, and the habit embeds itself more deeply (plus you might break something!!).

The way you use your mind makes permanent changes to the wiring of your brain (both positive and negative). If you let your mind roam free, you create wiring that makes it easy for your brain to be distracted every time you need to focus. If you practise the *Mind Gardener Method* you create wiring that enables your mind to be clear and present. Which one would you prefer? It's your choice.

Just like training for a sporting event, discipline is key. You may need to remind yourself every day of the importance of your mind exercises. Start your day as you wish it to continue. And find the opportunities to practise every day.

> it shouldn't be hard or painful!

No-one is striving for perfection here. The aim is not about reaching an end state, where you have a perfectly still mind 100 per cent of the time. That's just not realistic. Periods of being in the moment only endure for seconds, even with practice. The objective is not to 'stay' in the present, but to continuously 'return' to the present by using the practices. Sometimes when you practise focusing your attention on one thing, you will find that it will only be one second before you notice it wandering again. This is perfectly okay. The more times you become aware of this and switch your attention, the stronger your mind muscle gets!

The exercises are not about thought suppression. Any sign that you are using effort is a good indicator that you are not practising the techniques correctly. Arising thoughts are not the problem. It's the secondary step of grasping them and playing with them that makes us fall victim to our mindsets.

So don't try to stop your thoughts. When you have negative thoughts, don't beat yourself up and say 'I shouldn't be thinking that!' When you do this, you are still firing the same negative brain circuitry. Instead just acknowledge them and let them pass.

In a similar vein, remember that many of the mind exercises are about directing your flow of attention. With mindful exercises, you direct this flow through one of your senses. Many people forget this when they try practices like Mindful Listening. Instead of directing their attention to hearing, they *try* to listen. And when that doesn't work, they try even harder. Remember to simply and gently direct your attention.

> complacency creeps in

One of the biggest red flags is when someone says 'I've already got this'. It is important not to fall into the trap of believing that, because you have made personal gains, you have 'mastered' the practices! Let's face it, if you are still on this earth, you are not enlightened and are therefore not a master of your mind! Often the complacency from thinking you've 'got it' is revealed by a bad experience, where old issues arise and mindfulness is not able to be applied effectively. Never stop your practice.

Would you ever stop exercising because you've 'got it'? No, you would recognise that your fitness requires a regular invest-ment over your lifetime. Your mind fitness is the same. We have seen many people think they have a handle on things and stop practising. Within a week, the busy mind or destructive emotions begin to creep back in. Even though you may feel like a changed person, the old wiring is still there and can rear up if you are not vigilant.

You should also try to avoid allowing practices to become mindless habits, by regularly challenging yourself to uncover new mindsets and trying new ways of practising the *Mind Gardener Method*. It is worthwhile to take some time to reflect each week, and identify whether you are being as disciplined as you can be.

› don't doubt the simplicity of the method

Even when people know that the solution to their challenges rests in the mind, it is astounding how many will slip back into the trap of thinking they need to change a 'thing' in their life instead. Lucy was one of our clients who was constantly anxious about not finding a partner to share her life with. She was doing well using the *Mind Gardener Method*, but we ran into her some months later and we could see in her eyes that she was struggling. When we asked how she was going with the practices, she said it was going okay and she had started a new diet last week. As she kept talking, it was clear that the diet was not a result of seeing a need from a clear mind. It was just that changing her physical appearance was the old way she used to respond to the fear of not getting a guy. She had reverted back to this familiar strategy, forgetting that it had never worked!

Remember that your mind will throw up lots of excuses, designed to entice you back to your old patterns, mindsets and fears. We are used to finding complex solutions to our problems and sometimes mind training seems too simple to work. But it does work. This has been proven time and time again. So the important thing is to have faith and stick to your commitments. You'll see reassuring results pretty quickly.

> references

> chapter 1

1 Lyubomirsky, S (2008) *The How of Happiness: The Scientific Approach to Getting the Life You Want* New York, Penguin Press

> chapter 2

2 Maguire, E (2000) 'Navigation-related structural change in the hippocampi of taxi drivers.' *Proceedings of the National Academy of Sciences*, 97 (8), 4398–4403

3 Pascual-Leone A, Nguyet D, Cohen LG, Brasil-Neto JP, Cammarota A, Hallett M (1995) 'Modulation of muscle responses evoked by transcranial magnetic stimulation during the acquisition of new fine motor skills.' *Journal of Neurophysiology*, 74:1037–45

4 Ekman, P (1980) *Face of Man: Universal Expression in a New Guinea Village*. Garland, New York

> chapter 3

5 Takahashi, H, Kato, M, Matsuura, M., Mobbs, D, Suhara, T, Okubo, Y (2009), *When Your Gain Is My Pain and Your Pain is My Gain: Neural Correlates of Envy and Schadenfreude*. Science 13 February 2009: 937–939

6 Marmot, Sir M (2004) *The Status Syndrome: How Social Standing Affects Our Health and Longevity*. Owl Books

7 McEwen B, Lasley E (2004) *The End of Stress As We Know It*. Joseph Henry Press

8 Wills, AJ, Lavric, A, Croft, G.S, Hodgson, TL (2007), Predictive learning, prediction errors and attention: Evidence from event-related potentials and eye-tracking. *Journal of Cognitive Neuroscience*, *19*(5), 843–854

9 Moser, JS, Schroder, HS, Heeter, C, Moran, TP, Lee, Y-H (October 2011), Mind your errors: Evidence for a neural mechanism linking growth mindset to adaptive post-error adjustments, *Psychological Science*

10 Jordan, M (1994) *I Can't Accept Not Trying: Michael Jordan on the Pursuit of Excellence*. Harper Collins

11 Interview between *The Times* and Jonny Wilkinson (22 September 2008), promoting his book *Tackling Life: Striving for Perfection*. Headline Publishing Group

› chapter 4

12 Ellsberg, Daniel (1961). 'Risk, ambiguity and the savage axioms.' *Quarterly Journal of Economics*, 75(4): 643–669

13 Camerer, C and Weber, M (1992). 'Recent developments in modeling Preferences: uncertainty and ambiguity.' *Journal of Risk and Uncertainty*, 5(4): 325–37

14 Goleman, D and Boyatzis, R (September 2008) Social intelligence and the biology of leadership. *Harvard Business Review*

› chapter 5

15 Eisenberger, N and Lieberman M, with Williams, KD, 'Does rejection hurt? An fMRI study of social exclusion', *Science* Vol. 302 No. 5643, October 2003, 290–292

16 Rizzolatti, G and Sinigaglia, C (2008) *Mirrors in the Brain: How our Minds Share Actions, Emotions, and Experience* Oxford Press

17 Iyengar, S and Agrawal, K (2010) 'A better choosing experience', *Strategy + Business*, September 27, 2010

› chapter 6

18 Wilson, TD and Lassiter, G. D 'Increasing intrinsic interest with superfluous extrinsic constraints', *Journal of Personality and Social Psychology*, Vol 42(5), May 1982, 811–819

19 Christakis N and Fowler J (2009) *Connected: The Surprising Power of Our Social Networks and How They Shape Our Lives*, Little Brown

20 Research by Eldar Shafir of Princeton University and Sendhil Mullainathan of Harvard cited in *New York Times* on July 7, 2011

21 Moll J, Krueger F, Zahn R, Pardini M, de Oliveira-Souza R, Grafman J (2006), 'Human fronto-mesolimbic networks guide decisions about charitable donation.' *Proceedings of the National Academy of Sciences*

› chapter 7

22 www.peterhughesburnfoundation.org.au

23 Guth, Schmittberger and Schwarze (1982) 'An experimental analysis of ultimatum bargaining.' *Journal of Economic Behaviour and Organisation*, 3, 367–388

24 Sanfey AG, Rilling JK, Aronson JA, Nystrom LE and Cohen JD (2003) 'The neural basis of economic decision-making in the ultimatum game.' *Science*, 300, 1755–1758

25 Talwar, V, Gordon, HM, and Lee, K (2007). 'Lying in elementary school years: verbal deception and its relation to second-order belief understanding.' *Developmental Psychology, 43*, 804–810

› chapter 8

26 Davidson RJ, Kabat-Zinn J, Schumacher J, et al (2003) 'Alterations in brain and immune function produced by mindfulness meditation'. *Psychosomatic Med* 65 (4): 564–70

27 Kuhn, T (1962) *The Structure of Scientific Revolutions*. The University of Chicago Press

28 Stern Y, Albert S, Tang MX, et al (1999) 'Rate of memory decline in AD is related to education and occupation: cognitive reserve?' Neurology, 53: 1942–1957.

› chapter 9

29 Manhart, K (2004) 'The limits of multitasking'. *Scientific American Mind* December ed

› chapter 10

30 Shermer, M (2012) 'How we opt out of overoptimism: our habit of ignoring what is real is a double-edged sword'. *Scientific American Mind* March ed

31 Buckingham, M and Clifton, D (2001) *Now, Discover Your Strengths*. The Free Press

› resources

› life changing brain training programs

Mind Gardener® resources: a range of guides and programs to help you cultivate your mind:

www.mindgardener.com

Find us on **Facebook: Mind Gardener**

Find us on **Twitter: @mindgardentips**

› discipline

Once of the biggest challenges is simply to remember to practise your mind exercises. You can download something like the mindfulness bell that rings at specified or random intervals. Consider these:

Windows computer:

http://www.mindfulnessdc.org/mindfulclock.html

Android app, includes a vibrate option for those working in quiet environments

http://www.appbrain.com/app/mindfulness-bell/com. googlecode.mindbell

iPhone app, and other similar apps to help focus your mind

http://itunes.apple.com/us/app/mindfulness-bell/ id380816407?mt=8

› gratitude

Gratitude practices are some of the most popular mind training exercises, and keeping a Gratitude Journal has been identified as a powerful technique for stimulating happiness. Check out the Happy Tapper application for iPhone and iPad

www.happytapper.com

For motivation to be grateful every day, follow the 365 Grateful Project

www.365grateful.com

› strengths

Assess your signature strengths with the tests available at the University of Pennsylvania website dedicated to Dr Martin Seligman's work on positive psychology.

www.authentichappiness.sas.upenn.edu

› grow mental functions of the brain

There are now many web sites dedicated to tools, resources and games that promise to improve your brain. Just type "brain training" into your search engine to see if there are any that appeal to you. Game consoles like Nintendo also offer games that stretch the mind.

Try the crossword and sudoku in your daily newspaper.

Expose yourself to some of the most influential and fascinating people of our time by watching talks on many different topics who are invited to speak at TED.

www.ted.com

› know your brain

Find out more about your brain by subscribing to the Scientific American Mind magazine. This monthly magazine explores the latest brain science research and findings and discusses the implications in an accessible way. You can also sign up for their email newsletter.

www.scientificamerican.com/mind-and-brain

The Centre for Investigating Healthy Minds is located at the University of Wisconsin-Madison and is dedicated to rigorous research on positive qualities that make healthy minds flourish. Their site contains many resources and references.

www.investigatinghealthyminds.org

Where it all started for us: The Mind & Life Institute, building a scientific understanding of the mind to reduce suffering and promote wellbeing.

www.mindandlife.org

› find out more about the authors' work

www.wiredforlife.com.au
www.mindgardener.com
www.reinvention.com.au
Facebook: Mind Gardener
Twitter: @mindgardentips

> testimonials

'Susan and Martina are regular presenters and writers in our AusMumpreneur Network. They always have our members amazed by the power of the mind and that they have the power to literally 'change' the way they think. These new insights have changed lives and inspired people to implement the strategies and techniques explained by the ladies in both their personal and professional lives. I personally have found greater clarity, more innovative thinking and an increased sense of calm from working with the Mind Gardener team and I would highly recommend Wired for Life to anyone wanting to change their life by unlocking the power of their mind.'

Peace Mitchell, Co-director of Connect2mums &
The AusMumpreneur Network, Australia

'I have suffered with anxiety for well over 15 years, and through medication and counselling have mostly managed it well. I believe the Mind Gardener tools have been the missing link for me in my therapies, and using them has filled a gap that I could not explain. I always knew the gap existed, but until I started using the tools I did not realise how incomplete my therapies were, and in fact I have been amazed by how simple the tools are. I can say after using the exercises for six months, I am a much happier and more positive person. I cannot praise Mind Gardener enough. I even gave a copy of the tool to my psychiatrist. I know it is not designed for depression, however I believe this tool should be embraced by all health experts and support groups.'

John, 36, Melbourne

'Our firm wouldn't be where it is today without the insightful guidance of Martina and Susan. I'm always steadied by their presence, and they have an uncanny ability to engage even the toughest of lawyers! Theirs' is an important message for individuals and businesses who are prepared to think differently, and who believe in achieving success with meaning.'

Paul Spiro, Chairman Gadens Lawyers QLD, Australia

'Martina and Susan are a dynamic duo. They inspire me with the clarity they give around thinking and its impact and application. They effortlessly engage with their audience to deliver a refreshing take on how to change your life, one thought at a time. They truly are thought provoking!'

Paul Fairweather, creative catalyst, IDAES

> acknowledgements

> Susan:

To Jason, for putting my dreams above everything else, and giving me the love, encouragement and time for their pursuit. To Holly and Jack for providing more lessons than any other teacher. May you use the knowledge found in this book to achieve what is my greatest wish for you – a lifetime of happiness and fulfilment.

> Martina:

Thank you to both of my parents for being shining examples of unconditional love and acceptance. I could not have asked for better parents or a more nurturing childhood. My best qualities are a credit to you. My worst are simply bad habits I picked up when I wasn't listening to you!

> About the founders of Mind Gardener

Everything you think, learn, see and do shapes your brain and changes your life. You are a mind gardener.

> This is a message that has transformed the lives of people around the world and one that *Wired For Life* authors, Susan Pearse and Martina Sheehan have been spreading in both the business and personal development fields for decades.

Based in Brisbane, Susan and Martina are dedicated to making the science of the mind accessible to all. They explain how your brain shapes your life and what you can do to change it. By translating emerging neuroscience findings into simple knowledge, they reveal how to cultivate your mind and change your life, with simple exercises that can be done anytime, anywhere.

A chance meeting with His Holiness the Dalai Lama in 2003, cemented their resolve to spread the message about the potential of the mind, and show people how to develop the skill of mindfulness: an essential skill for living well in the modern world.

Their passion lies in helping cultivate the mind to improve performance, increase happiness, and live a life of purpose, fulfilment and success. The hundreds of testimonials they have received indicate they excel at it.

For more than a decade, Martina and Susan have introduced their mind gardening techniques into some of Australia's largest and most high profile businesses, via their consulting business *reinvention®*. In 2009, they succumbed to pleas from their clients, for tools to take home. They created the *Mind Gardener®* range, a series of step-by-step guides that make mind training easy. The best-selling *Mind Gardener*® range includes *The Living Happy Guide, The Clear Mind Guide, The Great Relationships Guide* and *The Bump to Baby Guide.*

Articles by *Mind Gardener*® have been published widely in national magazines. Susan and Martina have appeared on a variety of national television and radio programs, and are sought-after guest speakers. They continue to inspire audiences across Australia, with their entertaining style and thought provoking ideas.

Wired For Life is Martina and Susan's first book published by Hay House.

› Martina Sheehan

› Born in Melbourne in 1965, Martina has enjoyed a varied career, starting her working life as a mechanical engineer before moving into management roles in human resource management. She started her own strategic change consulting business in Brisbane in 1998, but it wasn't until meeting fellow mind fitness fanatic Susan Pearse, that she began integrating mind-cultivating techniques into her business. Assisting others to harness the potential of their minds is now her life's work.

Martina has been transforming organisations, leaders, and teams with ground-breaking brain-based development programs for over a decade. She has built a reputation for 'thinking differently' and she walks the talk. Her guidance has resulted in awards for her clients, and creates the sort of change that is sustainable. Her clients often say their experience was life changing.

Martina is recognised as a leader in the area of the mind and has been a keynote speaker at international conferences. She is called upon to guest lecture at Universities and has been featured in many radio, TV and media interviews.

Martina commits to a daily mind gardening practice and is a keen student of diverse fields of interest including philosophy, neuroscience and anthropology. When she is not pursuing her purpose, she is indulging her love of travel with her partner Phil.

› Susan Pearse

› Susan was born in Mackay in 1972 and moved to Brisbane in the early 1990s to undertake a business degree. While her background is in organisational change and leadership development, it wasn't until teaming up with Martina Sheehan that she discovered where her real passion lay – the power of the mind. Together they created their successful corporate consulting business *reinvention®*, which focuses on showing businesses how to think differently.

Susan has developed a reputation for changing the way people approach not only their business, but also their life. Many leaders credit Susan's insight and guidance as the key to uncovering a renewed sense of purpose and pursuing the balance, success and satisfaction that was missing from their life.

Susan regularly shares her tips for mindful living in the media, appearing in magazines, newspapers, documentaries and online. She is also a regular columnist and presenter for the AusMumpreneur Network.

Susan is on the Development Board of the Queensland Brain Institute, a world-leading organisation in brain research.

As a working mother and entrepreneur, Susan understands the challenges of juggling a busy career while maintaining a rewarding and fulfilling family life. She is a firm believer in practising what she preaches, and dedicates at least 30 minutes every day to exercising her mind. Susan lives in Brisbane with her husband Jason, and children Holly and Jack.

We hope you enjoyed this Hay House book. If you'd like to receive our online catalogue featuring additional information on Hay House books and products, or if you'd like to find out more about the Hay Foundation, please contact:

Hay House Australia Pty. Ltd.,
18/36 Ralph St., Alexandria NSW 2015
Phone: +61 2 9669 4299 • *Fax:* +61 2 9669 4144
www.hayhouse.com.au

Published and distributed in the USA by:
Hay House, Inc., P.O. Box 5100, Carlsbad, CA 92018-5100
Phone: (760) 431-7695 • *Fax:* (760) 431-6948
www.hayhouse.com®

Published and distributed in the United Kingdom by:
Hay House UK, Ltd., 292B Kensal Rd., London W10 5BE
Phone: 44-20-8962-1230 • *Fax:* 44-20-8962-1239
www.hayhouse.co.uk

Published and distributed in the Republic of South Africa by:
Hay House SA (Pty), Ltd., P.O. Box 990, Witkoppen 2068
Phone/Fax: 27-11-467-8904
www.hayhouse.co.za

Published in India by:
Hay House Publishers India, Muskaan Complex, Plot No. 3, B-2,
Vasant Kunj, New Delhi 110 070
Phone: 91-11-4176-1620 • *Fax:* 91-11-4176-1630
www.hayhouse.co.in

Distributed in Canada by:
Raincoast, 9050 Shaughnessy St., Vancouver, B.C. V6P 6E5
Phone: (604) 323-7100 • *Fax:* (604) 323-2600
www.raincoast.com

Take Your Soul on a Vacation
Visit **www.HealYourLife.com®** to regroup, recharge, and reconnect with your own magnificence. Featuring blogs, mind-body-spirit news, and life-changing wisdom from Louise Hay and friends.

Visit **www.HealYourLife.com®** today!

Made in the USA
San Bernardino, CA
04 January 2016